The PBIS Tier Two Handbook

The PBIS Tier Two Handbook

A Practical Approach to Implementing Targeted Interventions

Jessica Djabrayan Hannigan and John E. Hannigan

CORWIN
A SAGE Publishing Company

FOR INFORMATION:

Corwin
A SAGE Company
2455 Teller Road
Thousand Oaks, California 91320
(800) 233-9936
www.corwin.com

SAGE Publications Ltd.
1 Oliver's Yard
55 City Road
London EC1Y 1SP
United Kingdom

SAGE Publications India Pvt. Ltd.
B 1/I 1 Mohan Cooperative Industrial Area
Mathura Road, New Delhi 110 044
India

SAGE Publications Asia-Pacific Pte. Ltd.
3 Church Street
#10-04 Samsung Hub
Singapore 049483

Program Director: Jessica Allan
Associate Editor: Lucas Schleicher
Editorial Assistant: Mia Rodriguez
Production Editor: Tori Mirsadjadi
Copy Editor: Karin Rathert
Typesetter: C&M Digitals (P) Ltd.
Proofreader: Annie Lubinsky
Indexer: Nancy Fulton
Cover Designer: Michael Dubowe
Marketing Manager: Charline Maher

Printed in the United States of America

978-1-5063-8452-8

This book is printed on acid-free paper.

18 19 20 21 22 10 9 8 7 6 5 4 3 2 1

Contents

Preface

We wrote *The PBIS Tier Two Handbook* to accompany and extend the work of *The PBIS Tier One Handbook* published by Corwin Press. *The PBIS Tier One Handbook* provides a framework with practical steps for implementation for schools and districts establishing a Tier 1 (school-wide) behavior system. *The PBIS Tier Two Handbook* is framed to serve a similar purpose for implementing a Tier 2 behavior system. It will give the user a step-by-step framework based on effective implementation of Tier 2 interventions in over 400 schools across California. This book includes practical examples, case scenarios, and rubrics for identifying current states of implementation with tips to close gaps from recommended actions and examples. This book will also be used in teacher, support services, and administrator preparation programs and for professional development purposes for current educators/administrators. *The PBIS Tier One Handbook* and *The PBIS Tier Two Handbook* are designed to be interactive in nature during trainings.

CRITICAL TAKEAWAYS

This book is designed to help educators achieve three things at their schools:

1. Build on the Tier 1 behavior system of your school (addresses approximately 80 percent of students in a tiered behavior system).

2. Create a Tier 2 behavior response system with procedures and protocols that address targeted/at-risk behavior needs (addresses approximately 10 to 15 percent of students in a tiered behavior system).

3. Develop, audit, and implement a menu of Tier 2 interventions within this Tier 2 system based on student needs and data.

Note

You need all three to achieve sustainable behavioral outcomes at your school. The ultimate goal is to develop a tiered behavior system designed to respond to student social-emotional needs at each level of intensity. We often work with schools that have versions of Tier 2 interventions in place in pockets of the school (e.g., the school psychologist may offer a Tier 2 social skills group for a group of students), but there is no Tier 2 system designed with a menu of effective Tier 2 interventions understood by the administration and staff. In addition, the Tier 2 interventions are not accessible in a timely fashion nor are they implemented or monitored with fidelity. We also see schools who assign one type of Tier 2 intervention (e.g., Check-In Check-Out) as a catch-all for all students. This produces misconceptions from teachers and staff about the appropriate purpose of effective Tier 2 interventions based on student need.

In simple terms, think of it like this: If a person wants to lose weight because he is at-risk for health reasons, he will need a system to support his targeted plan for it to be successful. In order for the diet plan to work, this person needs to believe in the diet, set the household environment up for success with the diet, notify family and friends so they can help this person stay consistent, learn new skills and replacement behaviors, and monitor and track progress through reasonable goals and incentives for meeting his weight goals. Without this system and intentional plan to help him change behavior for the long term and generalize the learned behaviors in all settings, he could revert to having no change in weight or health outcomes.

This example is similar to a Tier 2 behavior system and selected targeted Tier 2 interventions provided within this framework. This will not work if you do not establish buy-in from the administration and staff, if no plan exists for meeting and discussing students who are at-risk, if needed skills are not being explicitly taught to your at-risk students, or if students don't feel success by setting reasonable SMART goals.

This book will ensure you have established a Tier 2 system that will support your school's Tier 2 intervention needs and will serve as a guide to reflect on your current practices and enhance them to attain the best outcomes for students who need additional supports beyond Tier 1.

Acknowledgments

Implementing effective tiered systems of social-emotional supports for students is critical for their success in school and beyond. In working with schools and districts throughout the nation, we identified this area as a need for educators and practitioners. Investing in this work is what is equitable for *all* students; hence the premise of this book.

We wish to first acknowledge the outstanding professionals at the schools and districts we train and support. We have had the privilege of working with some of the finest educators and students in America. Thank you to the following organizations for their contributions to our inspiration and knowledge in creating this book: Fresno County Office of Education; California State University, Fresno; Center for Leadership Equity and Research (CLEAR); Fix School Discipline Coalition; California Endowment; and Sanger Unified School District. Also, to all our supervisors, mentors, professors, colleagues, students, friends and family who have given us the platform to innovate and have shared in this passion of what we believe in. This would not have been possible without all of you.

To the Djabrayan and Hannigan families, we thank you for your endless love, support, and encouragement. A special thank you to our parents Bedros and Dzovinar Djabrayan and Mike and Sky Hannigan for your help and relentless support during this process.

To our gorgeous girls, Riley and Rowan, thank you for all your love and encouragement. To our son, John Edward Hannigan V, thank you for being a blessing and our inspiration. Through our work, we hope to model for you what it means to have a strong work ethic and to help others in whatever future career paths you pursue.

Our appreciation to the team at Corwin for recognizing this as a comprehensive and innovative method for addressing inequities in schools. Thank you again for giving us the platform to share our voice and help students.

To all who read this book, we thank you for truly having the courage and passion to do what is best for *all* students.

PUBLISHER'S ACKNOWLEDGMENTS

Corwin gratefully acknowledges the contributions of the following reviewers:

Gloria Avolio, PhD
school counselor instructional mentor
Hillsborough County Public Schools
Tampa, FL

Julie Frederick
nationally board certified kindergarten teacher
Seattle Public Schools
Seattle, WA

Vikki Kelly
instructor, special education/language arts
Carroll Middle School
Southlake, TX

Pamela Nevills, EdD
instructor, author
Brandman University
Irvine, CA

Brigitte Tennis
educator and headmistress
Stella Schola Middle School
Redmond, WA

About the Authors

Dr. Jessica Djabrayan Hannigan is an assistant professor in the Educational Leadership Department at California State University, Fresno. She has extensive experience in P–12 general education and special education administration at the school and district level. She also works as an educational consultant, training approximately 500 schools across the country on implementing effective and equitable academic and behavior systems in schools and districts. She currently serves as a member of the Center for Leadership, Equity, and Research (CLEAR) and the Fix School Discipline Coalition.

Dr. John E. Hannigan is principal of Reagan Elementary in the Sanger Unified School District in California. He has served in education for 15 years as a principal, assistant principal, instructional coach, and teacher. Dr. Hannigan specializes in building strong school cultures, developing leaders at all levels, and creating effective academic and behavior systems. Under his leadership, his school has received numerous awards and recognitions, including California State Distinguished School, Gold Ribbon School, Title I Academic School, and Positive Behavioral Interventions and Supports (gold level), and has been recognized as an exemplary Response to Intervention (RTI) school for both academics and behavior. His school was selected as a knowledge development site for the statewide scaling up of Multi-Tiered Systems of Support (MTSS). He currently serves as a member of the Center for Leadership, Equity, and Research (CLEAR).

Before You Begin

How to Use *The PBIS Tier Two Handbook*

THE PBIS TIER TWO HANDBOOK

The Why? There is a need for schools to build social-emotional systems designed to respond to students exhibiting at-risk/targeted behavior needs. There are inequities in school discipline; specifically for students of color and special education students.

The How? *The PBIS Tier Two Handbook* is designed to provide a framework for educators to create a Tier 2 system that incorporates a menu of Tier 2 interventions available for students in need of targeted behavior interventions.

The What? Educators learn how to implement the ABCs of Tier 2. Practical examples and guidance are provided to help educators create a system that fits their school's needs. Educators will learn how to design and audit Tier 2 behavior interventions based on the needs and data of their schools or districts.

WHAT IS THIS BOOK DESIGNED TO HELP YOU DO?

This book is designed to help educators continue the development of their tiered behavior systems in their school or district. Specifically, this book focuses on designing a system that responds to Tier 2 behavior intervention needs. So . . . What does this look like? What does it sound like? How will we know if the Tier 2 interventions are working or not? The intended outcome for the development of this book is for educators to use this framework to design a menu of effective at-risk/targeted behavior interventions as a guide to establishing a tight Tier 2 behavior system tailored to fit your individual school's needs.

In working with a large number of schools, we have identified a need in this area. We have noticed a tendency for some schools to lean toward a "one size fits all" approach to Tier 2 interventions and/or misconceptions about what Tier 2 interventions need in order to be effective. Our aim is to help educators make the connection that designing tiered systems of support for students who struggle behaviorally are supported with the same attention, focus, and patience as are students who struggle academically. **Consider this:** If we have a group of students in need of a literacy focused intervention in the area of phonics, we would not provide them with a fluency intervention. We would identify the specific phonics rules lacking and provide a specific, targeted phonics intervention to close this gap. We would then progress monitor to see how the students are responding to the intervention. If the students are responding, we continue the intervention; if the students are not, we change the intervention and continue progress monitoring before increasing the intensity of the intervention.

However, is this the typical response for students who struggle with their behavior? We've seen all too frequently schools who use the same one or two common Tier 2 interventions year after year to serve the varying needs of their students demonstrating Tier 2 intervention needs rather than establishing and implementing targeted interventions based on the data, the needs of the students, and/or the needs of their school or district. Oftentimes, accurate data are not collected or reviewed in a structured method by a behavior or leadership team designed to address the targeted intervention needs of the students and staff.

Without critical markers and characteristics in place, such as the few mentioned in this section, your school has work to do in creating, refining, and sustaining an effective Tier 2 behavior system. This book is designed to build on the foundation of *The PBIS Tier One Handbook* and (1) create a system to respond to Tier 2 behavior intervention needs, (2) help Tier 2 behavior teams identify targeted behavior intervention needs of the school, (3) help Tier 2 behavior teams establish targeted behavior interventions with all critical markers and characteristics in place, and (4) implement and monitor with fidelity the Tier 2 intervention SMART goals.

When your Tier 2 behavior sub-team identifies a trend in at-risk behaviors based on data and stakeholder input, it is essential to establish a targeted intervention to address the needs in a timely fashion. For example, if the team notices a bullying challenge, an increase in hands-on behavior, repeated minor disruptions in the classroom, motivation, tardies, or more, an intervention must be put in place to address it promptly.

HOW CAN TIER 2 BEHAVIOR INTERVENTIONS BENEFIT YOUR STUDENTS?

Tier 2 Intervention Implementation Celebrations: Quotes From Educators

"Jason was a student who couldn't keep his hands to himself. He had a history of being suspended for the same behavior. After participating in the Hands Off Academy Tier 2 intervention provided at our school, he became a mentor for younger students demonstrating similar behaviors."

"Check-In Check-Out helped Melvin tremendously this school year. It helped me help him become successful in my class. I started noticing he was more on task and less disruptive. Prior to Check-In Check-Out, he received all Fs, and during his participation, his GPA improved to a C average and I did not feel the need to dismiss him from class on a daily basis."

"Michelle's tardies improved after participating in the tardy project intervention. Prior to this intervention, Michelle was consistently late to every period. Through this Tier 2 intervention, she learned the time management and organizational skills she lacked to help her become successful."

"Social Skills group was very helpful for both Billy and Jay. These two boys were struggling every day during unstructured times. After learning how to appropriately gain peer attention, they discovered better methods of making friends rather than trying to show off by getting into trouble."

"Friendship group made a huge difference in the online bullying that was taking place amongst a group of girls at my school. Specifically, the girls who participated in this Tier 2 intervention learned empathy skills and how to show compassion towards other students. Most importantly, they learned how to co-exist in the school environment and online. Part of this intervention required them to implement online bully prevention efforts at not only their school but at other neighboring elementary schools as well. The feedback from the elementary schools was positive and well received by the students. In addition, they had to create parent workshops on the topic of how parents can identify and help with online bullying."

"Our school was in need of a motivation intervention for a handful of students who were not necessarily behavior problems, but they did not complete any work in their classes. As a result, they were being suspended

from class, further resulting in them getting behind. After participating in this motivation intervention, they gained the skills needed to organize, not become overwhelmed, communicate their challenges, and ask for help."

We also want to intentionally note that this book is designed to help educators with their Tier 2 system at their school no matter what programs or initiatives they prefer to implement school-wide. For example, if a school or district wants to focus on restorative practices primarily, then they can utilize this book to help create a system of restorative practices at the Tier 2 targeted level. This applies to Character Education, Trauma Informed Practices, Culturally Responsive Practices, and so forth. The ultimate goal is that schools have a structured format for adding additional layers of tiered support for students who require more time, more skills, and more support in any way that addresses their social-emotional needs. This book is also designed to make sure a process is in place to monitor and adjust effectiveness of interventions and implementation.

Our framework is referred to as the PBIS Champion Model; however, we want to emphasize this does not mean our frame does not have the flexibility to include other effective programs and initiatives as part of the tiered system we are helping educators design. In fact, we highly recommend the use of best practices. Our goal is to help you evaluate, organize, and refine your systems in a method that can be sustainable and replicable for other schools and districts. One misconception is that this framework is in competition with other initiatives. What makes this framework unique is that we encourage the use of other programs that help you meet your intervention goals. We understand some PBIS models do not allow for an interconnection of initiatives, which makes the Champion Model a unique vehicle to help connect and enhance existing and new initiatives based on your desired outcomes for *all* students.

This book encourages a collaborative and practical approach to designing and monitoring Tier 2 behavior interventions. Here are the most commonly asked questions and answers as you begin designing a school system that responds to at-risk/targeted behaviors of students.

FREQUENTLY ASKED QUESTIONS

Should we have implemented *The PBIS Tier One Handbook* before we begin implementation of *The PBIS Tier Two Handbook?*

Best practice would be to implement *The PBIS Tier One Handbook* at your school first. *The PBIS Tier One Handbook* will build the school-wide behavior foundation for your school. If Tier 1 is in place with fidelity, you will have fewer students requiring at-risk/targeted behavior interventions at your school. Additionally, working through *The PBIS Tier One Handbook* will help your team understand the framework of the PBIS Champion Model. If you already have a strong Tier 1 behavior system in place, utilize *The PBIS Tier One Handbook* to continue to refine and improve your existing systems.

What is the difference between markers, characteristics, and SMART goals outlined in this book?

In each tier of the PBIS Champion Model (Tier 1, Tier 2, Tier 3), there are established markers, characteristics, and SMART goals designed to help implementation at each level. Markers are critical components necessary to build the system at each level, Characteristics are defined as what the implementation would look and sound like, and SMART goals are designed to identify if the interventions are working or not.

What do we do with discipline in the meantime?

Utilize *Don't Suspend Me!: An Alternative Discipline Toolkit* to help you address behavior using an alternative/restorative approach. However, once again, we encourage you to continue visiting your Tier 1 foundation at your school (e.g., active supervision, classroom management, routines/procedures during structured and unstructured times, establishing relationships and connections with students).

How long does this take to implement?

It depends on the current state of the school or district. If the school or district is ready to implement and has a strong foundation in place for Tier 1, it usually takes the school year to begin developing, implementing, progress monitoring, and refining Tier 2 interventions.

Are the examples in the book real-life examples?

Yes, this book is written by practitioners for practitioners based on real-life situations and challenges brought up to the authors. Keep in mind, the examples are from schools at different levels of implementation. The idea is to share the most common challenges brought to our attention and provide easy-to-use practical solutions and templates as a guide.

Who implements these Tier 2 interventions?

It depends. We suggest you conduct a simple human resources inventory. We challenge you to look at using some human resources differently. For example, take some things off the staff's plates, develop possible extra work agreements, and so forth. Remember, the tighter your Tier 1 system, the less students will need additional interventions.

Are Tier 2 interventions reserved only for special education students?

No, this is a huge misconception. Although you might have some special education students needing Tier 2 interventions, that does not necessarily mean that general education students who are in need of additional behavioral supports do not receive them.

What if the parents or guardians say no to the Tier 2 intervention?

We highly recommend that your tiered system of support is articulated in both the district and school handbooks indicating that students will be provided with additional tiered supports in academics and behavior as determined by the educators serving them. Of course, permission for any level of special education testing for behavior or academic services is required; however, there are always ways to provide supports for *all* students. Work with your school psychologist and district office to assist with those decisions. A collaborative relationship with the parent or guardian is always helpful when working to establish buy-in and trust. It is rare for a student to display disruptive behaviors only in the school environment. Typically, if these behaviors are frequent enough to need increasingly intensive supports at school, the parents are seeing these behaviors at home as well (even if they tell you they aren't). They want to see that the school is showing patience and support when dealing with their child's behavior. Parents push back when they see that the school is frustrated with their child and/or not doing enough to support the child. If the Tier 2 intervention requires a parent or guardian check-in component but it is not taking place because of the unavailability of that parent or guardian, select a teacher or other staff member who can be a Tier 2 intervention information surrogate for that student.

What if the student will not attend?

The intervention cannot be optional for the student. It is critical to connect with the student and make sure he understands the purpose of the intervention. Also, work with the student if he does not feel comfortable in a group intervention setting. Just because it is a Tier 2 intervention does not mean it can only be delivered in a small group setting. If the student continuously does not attend with all the supports provided, it may be time to consider a more individualized intervention or re-evaluate if this Tier 2 intervention is appropriate for this student.

Can a student stay in a Tier 2 intervention after the six to eight weeks if she has met the goals but seems to need it?

Some students need the ongoing adult interaction, reinforcement, and structures aligned with Tier 2 interventions. If a student is responding and continues to the need the support, continue the support; however, work on building their skills and confidence and begin to wean them off the Tier 2 intervention (e.g., maybe twice a week, to once a week, to twice a month instead of weekly).

Can some students skip Tier 2 interventions and go right into a Tier 3 intervention?

There are cases of students who need the individualized/intensive supports immediately as they come into a new setting or are struggling with a traumatic or serious emotional challenge. In these cases, work with the professionals who are experts in social-emotional supports in your school or district to ensure the student is safe and has stable supports in place for success. Please do not put a student who is in crisis and in need of immediate Tier 3 intensive interventions in a six- to eight-week Tier 2 intervention simply for the sake of reaching another level in a sequence of increasingly intensive supports to show the student isn't responding. Make sure to work with all stakeholders to decide on what is best for the student.

How do I get the teachers to buy into the Tier 2 intervention?

You will have to articulate the importance of the Tier 2 intervention so your teachers understand its value. Progress will not happen overnight, but your teachers will want to see immediate results. Be empathetic and highlight the successes they are having with the student because of their intentional implementation of an appropriate Tier 2 intervention. Make the connection to a student who struggles academically that will need increasingly intensive support to close the gap in learning; so too does a student who struggles to behave. Understand, misbehavior is typically met with frustration and sometimes anger from a teacher, while a student who struggles academically is usually met with compassion and extra support. The two responses cannot be mutually exclusive. Allow for the teacher to provide input and feedback into the Tier 2 intervention process, challenges, and successes. Make sure the implementation component is practical and easy to put into action while teaching a classroom of students. Include a Tier 2 update in each staff meeting or in professional development opportunities so the teachers understand how the Tier 2 system works.

When should Tier 2 interventions take place?

It depends on the school's leadership. If it is made a priority that Tier 2 interventions are a must and the interventions are protected with consistent times for implementation that are agreed upon by all stakeholders, then it should not be an issue. Some schools prefer implementation to take place before school, during unstructured times, after school, a designated secondary class period, Saturday school, and so forth. It really depends on the behavior team and the leadership of the school.

Note: It is important to make sure the selected time is utilized efficiently and students receive any missed class content.

Do Tier 2 interventions need to be offered outside of the classroom?

It depends on the Tier 2 intervention and the need of the students. Many Tier 2 interventions are best served in collaboration with the teachers and staff working with the students inside and out of the classroom setting to encourage the students to generalize their newly learned skills in multiple settings.

Some possible examples include the following:

Tier 2 Interventions (in Classroom Setting)	Tier 2 Interventions (out of Classroom Setting)
• Small group re-teaching • Review of classroom expectations and rules respect contracts • Individual check-in system • Break card system • Parent/guardian and school communication system • Check-In Check-Out (CICO) • Social stories • Classroom contract • Classroom circles	• Social skills • Structured recess • Hands Off Academy • Bully prevention • Organizational skills • Friendship groups • Anger management • Motivational skills • Check and connect • Restorative circles • Peer mediation

MOST COMMONLY ASKED QUESTION

Why Should Naughty Students Receive Incentives?

Creating effective behavior systems within schools requires multiple strategies that all student behaviors respond to. The majority of students will respond to a solid Tier 1 school-wide behavior system and incentives (see *The PBIS Tier One Handbook*); however, some students will require more to correct behavior. In these cases, Tier 2 (targeted/small-group) interventions are necessary. Students who meet a set of criteria for additional interventions (meaning Tier 1 systems are in place with fidelity but the individual student is not responding) need to have additional opportunities provided for them in order to learn the appropriate ways to behave.

We have experienced educators who do not believe students needing additional interventions should be incentivized for meeting their goals. We frequently hear the following comments: Why should a naughty student receive an incentive? Why is he being rewarded for behaving the way the other students *always* do? What do I tell the rest of my class seeing this student with a history of misbehavior receive an incentive for behaving the way they are supposed to? What we ask those educators is simple; how is it currently working out for you? Is the student responding to what you are currently doing? If you don't have a positive answer to either of these questions, then the response for that student needs to be changed. Here are three reasons why it is critical to educate staff on the importance of providing appropriate incentives for students responding to Tier 2 interventions.

Reason 1: *Choosing incentives that the student wants to earn is key.* Identifying what motivates the student as an incentive will help the student buy into the intervention. This does not necessarily have to be something tangible; some students ask for time with adults or other special privileges that can be free of cost (e.g., lunch with an administrator, time to draw, etc.). Whatever the incentive is, it must be something the student states that they want and not something the teacher or administrator thinks the student would like. Positive incentives for meeting Tier 2 intervention goals need to be consistent and meaningful for the student.

Reason 2: *Establishing relationships with the students will help shape their behavior.* During the time students receive incentives for meeting their goals, they are establishing relationships with the adults supporting them. It is important for the incentives to be consistent and for the student to feel assured that she can trust the adult's word. The terms of the incentive cannot be changed during the intervention or if the student meets their goal; the bar cannot be raised without first rewarding the student for meeting their goal. This will erode the trust in the adult and the process for the student and they will stop working toward their goal.

Reason 3: *Creating an opportunity for students to feel success with the intervention is essential to helping shape behavior.* Students need to be given an attainable goal aligned with the Tier 2 intervention that is monitored for effectiveness. It is important for the student to feel successful in meeting his goals. As the student feels success in attaining his new skills, he will begin generalizing the new behaviors in different settings. Look at the data to establish if the student is responding. If he is responding, reward the student, increase the goal, and reduce the intensity; if he is not responding, change the intervention and/or increase the intensity.

Educate your staff on the purpose and goal of putting a Tier 2 intervention in place using the provided reasons. Emphasize the goal of a Tier 2 intervention is for the student to practice behaving in the way that is expected.

This is not going to happen overnight, and it is not going to happen by continuing to do what hasn't worked in the past. Also consider, home circumstances differ for every student. Some students will not have experiences at home that give them a structured environment, while others will have tight procedures and expectations to follow. These students will bring those behaviors to your campus. They need to practice the appropriate ways to behave and in doing so, need to be rewarded when they are successful. The school's reward for taking the time to implement Tier 2 interventions with fidelity is a campus where every student behaves the way that is expected. Remember, the goal in Tier 2 is to get the student back in Tier 1 and off your radar, especially if that means giving an incentive to encourage them getting there.

What are some questions you may have?

_____

_____

_____

_____

_____

_____

_____

_____

_____

_____

Part I
Overview

The PBIS
Champion Model

The behavioral needs of a student should be addressed with the same level of focus and attention as their academic needs. You cannot have one without the other, if we are to educate the whole child, especially if our ultimate goal is to prepare students for college and a career. It is hard to argue the importance between instructional time and academic achievement; therefore, our top priority in education should be to keep students in class and engaged in learning to the greatest degree possible. Students who cannot demonstrate appropriate social skills will struggle tremendously, if we focus our efforts only on their academics while failing to address their critical behavioral needs. "Targeted" behavior supports are to be provided for students displaying occasional signs of mild to moderate at-risk misbehavior. Students in need of targeted supports can be identified more easily and their needs or behavior can be addressed more effectively when Tier 1, school-wide supports are soundly in place.

Positive Behavior Interventions and Supports (PBIS) is growing exponentially as a term, although not so much in its application or practice. PBIS has received negative pushback in some schools and districts, not so much because of the ineffectiveness of PBIS but rather the ineffectiveness of the *implementation* of PBIS in those places. PBIS, where implemented at a very surface level (albeit by well-intended individuals), has been negatively viewed by staff as being only banners, tickets, and incentives, with the lack of accountability or discipline. Time after time, we run into teachers with a very negative view of PBIS; teachers see the results of ineffective implementation as a reflection of the system rather than its implementation. If all ten markers in *The PBIS Tier One Handbook* are not in place, you are not doing PBIS. Also, don't get caught up with the semantics. Call it what you want (i.e., Response to Intervention [RTI] behavior or Multi-Tiered System of Supports [MTSS] behavior), but the question remains: Do you have a system of multiple, increasingly intensive tiers of support for students who struggle with their behavior?

The PBIS Champion Model, as a framework, is designed to help educators work together through a problem-solving model to provide an equitable education; support academic and behavior needs in a systematic way that addresses the needs of *all* students; and align the entire system of initiatives, supports, and resources; while implementing continuous improvement processes across all levels of the system. How do we do this in our schools? Where do we start? How do we strengthen our implementation of existing systems to address all of these components?

You will need to assess your current state prior to beginning this work. Most decisions within this framework are made by teams (site leadership teams, student support teams, or grade-level teams). To assess your current state and to ensure coherence throughout your system, work with a wide representation of staff/team members in your school across multiple grade levels using the following process: Ask each of the selected team members to list all initiatives/interventions in each tier provided for both the academic and behavior systems in your school. *Note:* This also includes Special Education, Gifted/Gate, English Language Development, etc. After the list is created, answer the following questions as a team for each item listed:

Who? (Criteria to get in and out, which students are served?)

What? (What do the students receive in the intervention?)

How? (Who is delivering the intervention? How often?)

Measured? (How is the intervention monitored for effectiveness/fidelity? How often?)

When at least 80 percent of your staff staff can clearly articulate the response to these four questions within each intervention or initiative implemented in all three tiers, then your school will be on the right track for creating tiered systems that will sustain and align to this framework. This process will inform your system as to where adequate training/support is needed as well as where to refine and enhance based on the continuous monitoring through the use of accurate data. Creating a behavior system aligned with this framework will take time and hard work. The work is never done; it will require ongoing effort based on the needs of your school. In order for this type of systematic framework to succeed, implementation and nurturing of the academic/behavior systems in the school need to be a top priority. Academic and behavior systems are very connected; you can't focus on one and not the other. Therefore, the PBIS Champion Model will enhance your system to support *all* students.

The PBIS Champion Model is a comprehensive systems approach for the design and delivery of PBIS in a school. This action-oriented framework provides *quality criteria* and *how-to steps* for developing, implementing, monitoring, and sustaining each level of the system: Bronze (Tier 1), Silver (Tier 2), and Gold (Tier 3). Each tier in the system consists of three categories: Category A—markers, Category B—characteristics, and Category C—academic and behavioral goals, and the work of the PBIS Team. Each category is composed of quality criteria and a set of defined actions. A brief overview of the quality criteria for each tier is provided with a quick glimpse of what a Champion Model school looks like in each level (Bronze, Silver, and Gold).

Figure 1.1

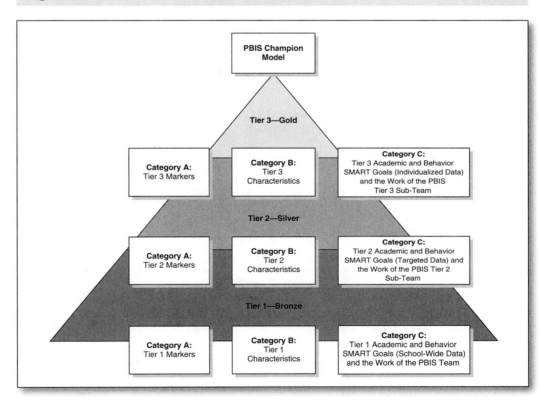

From our experience, most school administrators/staff indicate their school has some degree of a system in place to reactively respond to a student's behavior challenges, but many concede that they struggle implementing effective Tier 2 and Tier 3 behavior systems. The PBIS Champion Model Framework will help you gather baseline information and provide a set of criteria for establishing effective tiered systems in your school. Answer the following questions based on your school's current state as a baseline:

Can the school administration/staff articulate the importance of connecting academics and behavior when working with students? Explain:

_____

_____

_____

Are similar resources allocated to both academic and behavioral supports? Explain:

_____

_____

_____

Can the administration/staff articulate what is expected of them at the classroom level (Tier 1) as they are providing academic supports? Explain:

_____

_____

_____

Can the administration/staff articulate what is expected of them at the classroom level (Tier 1) as they are providing behavioral supports? Explain:

_____

_____

_____

Can the administration/staff articulate what is available for targeted or at-risk (Tier 2) academic interventions at the school for students not responding to the classroom supports alone? Explain:

_____

_____

_____

Can the administration/staff articulate what is available for targeted or at-risk (Tier 2) behavioral interventions at the school for students not responding to the classroom supports alone? Explain:

_____

_____

_____

Can the administration/staff articulate what is available for individualized (Tier 3) academic interventions (general education and special education) at the school for students not responding to the classroom level or targeted/at risk levels of intervention? Explain:

_____

_____

_____

Can the administration/staff articulate what is available for individualized (Tier 3) behavioral interventions (general education and special education) at the school for students not responding to the classroom level or targeted/at risk levels of intervention? Explain:

_____

_____

_____

Having a solid, preventive Tier 1 behavior system in place (see *The PBIS Tier One Handbook*) for a comprehensive guide, coupled with an innovative response to students who misbehave (see *Don't Suspend Me!: An Alternative Discipline Toolkit*) will be critical for the success of the work in this book.

Ask yourself this question: **Do you have the ABCs of PBIS Tier 1 implementation in place?** If the answer to this question is No or you do not know what the ABCs of PBIS Tier 1 are, utilize *The Tier One Handbook* to build your foundation first, before delving into Tier 2 markers for the best outcomes.

Why is this recommended? Through our professional experience of working with schools on implementation of both academic and behavior RTI, MTSS, and tiered-school interventions in general, we can say with confidence that if PBIS/the PBIS Champion Model is not implemented with fidelity in each tier, it will result in insufficient Tier 2 interventions, with too many students overidentified as needing them. Often, we find this is connected to inadequate leadership, fixed beliefs regarding discipline, and/or ineffective school systems (academic/behavior) missing critical key markers of implementation. Without a foundation of Tier 1 in place, you will encounter the following most common red flags, which will negatively impact your implementation of an effective Tier 2 system.

Here are the leading red flags connected with poor PBIS implementation:

PBIS referred to as a program—If PBIS is referred to as a program, the perception from the teachers and staff will be "this too shall pass." PBIS needs to be referred to as the behavior side of the school system; behavior RTI.

Lack of administrator buy-in—Administrators who do not believe in the fundamental markers necessary to implement a comprehensive behavior system will produce a staff who does not believe in the fundamental markers and will quickly return to the old way of responding to misbehavior—the easier way. Another common buy-in error is an administrator assuming everything is already being done with fidelity at their school when it is not. This is the toughest red flag to address, because it can involve bruised egos and difficult conversations. It also requires intervention from the district office or an immediate supervisor to ensure the administrator knows implementation is not optional, and even the best school systems need to continuously assess and improve.

Administrators not understanding all tiers of implementation— Administrators who do not understand the complexity of implementation in each tier (school-wide, targeted/at-risk, and individualized) struggle to build and sustain PBIS at model levels. We commonly see principals send other site representatives to trainings and/or PBIS team meetings while they themselves cannot fully articulate the system they are hoping to design and implement.

Teacher and staff misunderstanding of PBIS implementation— If teachers and staff are not properly trained on the markers of implementation, the goals and outcomes of implementation, and the reasons for why it is necessary to implement, they will have a shallow understanding of what PBIS means. A shallow understanding will produce those who refer to PBIS as only tickets, incentives, banners, and no discipline. If a staff defines PBIS only in this way, it is evident they do not understand that PBIS is an RTI behavior framework.

Lack of appropriate communication with staff about alternative discipline—When teachers and staff are not supported adequately with discipline, they will blame PBIS for not punishing students. This is a game-changing red flag and indicates the following:

- Collaboration and communication is not taking place with regard to discipline in a timely manner
- The expectation and culture of the school has still not shifted to the belief of helping *all* students learn and behave

To reiterate, in most cases, it is not PBIS that is not working, it is the *implementation* of PBIS that is not working. Tighten up implementation of Tier 1 before moving on to Tier 2 for the best outcomes.

The What and Why of a PBIS Tier 2 System

Creating effective behavior systems in schools requires multiple strategies that all student behaviors respond to. The majority of students will respond to a solid Tier 1 school-wide behavior system (see *The PBIS Tier One Handbook)*; however, some students will require more to correct behavior. In these cases, Tier 2 (targeted/at-risk) interventions or Tier 3 (individualized) interventions are necessary. Students who meet set criteria for additional interventions (meaning Tier 1 systems are in place with fidelity, but the individual student is not responding) need to have additional opportunities provided for them to learn the appropriate ways to behave. A Tier 2 intervention is commonly defined as an intervention for students demonstrating the need for targeted/at-risk behavioral supports and skills delivered in a small group or individualized fashion. The ultimate goal of providing a Tier 2 intervention is to prevent the student behaviors from escalating to a more intense level. Approximately 10 to 15 percent of the students in your school may need some level of a Tier 2 intervention. This definition alone does not break down the complex criteria and steps necessary for creating, implementing, and monitoring an effective Tier 2 intervention—hence, the purpose of the PBIS Champion Model Silver Level framework (Figure 2.1).

Figure 2.1

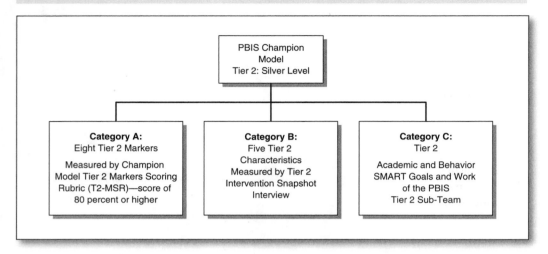

So what would you see if you visited a Silver Level PBIS Champion Model School and observed staff implementing one of their Tier 2 interventions? Based on your current knowledge, is School Environment A or School Environment B a Silver Level PBIS Champion Model School? Which school environment would you prefer to be a part of?

School Environment A	School Environment B
• Staff are frustrated with repeated student behaviors. • Staff do not know how to ask for help with students misbehaving. • There is only one Tier 2 intervention offered (e.g., social skills group), but it is full most of the school year. • It takes months before getting students into a Tier 2 intervention. • While in the intervention, the stakeholders are not communicated with or provided updates on student progress. • A school team has not been identified to improve Tier 2 interventions at the school. • Discipline is out of control.	• Staff feel challenged at times with student behavior, but the majority are ready to put in the extra time to help students. • Staff understand the process of requesting Tier 2 intervention supports for students. • There is an established PBIS Tier 2 sub-team that meets at least twice a month to address Tier 2 needs of the school. • There is one comprehensive Tier 2 intervention in place at the school based on the behavioral data (e.g., Hands Off Academy) • Tier 1 is in place with fidelity. • Students are placed into the intervention in a timely fashion. • The PBIS Tier 2 sub-team is working to develop a menu of comprehensive Tier 2 interventions for students.

School Environment A	School Environment B
• Staff are burned out. • Student behaviors are escalating. • Suspensions are the most common intervention used. • Behavior is not taught to students. • Students are lacking the social-emotional skills needed to succeed. • Staff are not equipped to provide the students with these skills. • Tier 1 behavior systems are not in place with fidelity. • Too many students are in need of Tier 2 interventions. • There are not enough resources to help with the interventions. • Incentives are not given to students for making progress.	• Data collected is aligned with the Tier 2 intervention SMART goals. • Student data is collected and shared with all stakeholders. • Opportunities are provided for feedback from the stakeholders when the interventions are not working. • Funding is available for weekly incentives for students meeting their Tier 2 intervention goals. • The administrators and support staff are in full support and part of the PBIS Tier 2 sub-team. • The Tier 2 intervention provides teaching opportunities for the students. • Students are given opportunities to generalize their learned skills in multiple settings. • All stakeholders provide students with positive feedback when they meet their goals. • Staff understand the concepts and importance of Tier 2 interventions. • Tier 2 intervention updates are provided to the entire staff at least monthly at staff meetings.

Much like School Environment B, you would see evidence of the eight critical Tier 2 markers, the five Tier 2 characteristics, and the established Tier 2 academic and behavior SMART goals with data evidencing progress of the students and effectiveness of the Tier 2 intervention.

☙❧

What is your school's current state in relation to School Environment A and School Environment B?

_____

_____

_____

_____

☙❧

WHAT ARE THE TIER 2 MARKERS, CHARACTERISTICS, AND SMART GOALS?

TIER 2
Markers

Marker 1: Establish and Operate an Effective PBIS Tier 2 Sub-Team
Marker 2: Establish and Maintain Tier 2 Staff Commitment
Marker 3: Establish a Tier 2 Data Based Process for Identifying Students
Marker 4: Establish a Tier 2 Data Entry Procedure and Review Plan
Marker 5: Establish a Tier 2 Fidelity Check Process
Marker 6: Develop and Deliver Tier 2 Lesson Plans
Marker 7: Establish a Tier 2 Behavior Incentive System
Marker 8: Establish a Tier 2 System for Monitoring and Communicating Progress

TIER 2
Characteristics

Characteristic 1: Existence of Criteria and Timely Referral Process

Characteristic 2: Visibility of Tier 2 Intervention Schedule

Characteristic 3: Evidence of Behavior Lessons and Social Skills

Characteristic 4: Existence of Academic/Behavior Goals/Incentives

Characteristic 5: Plan for Progress Monitoring/Communication

TIER 2
Academic and Behavior SMART Goals

SMART Goal Academic: A Tier 2 academic goal is a targeted/at-risk intervention academic SMART (Strategic and Specific, Measurable, Attainable/Achievable, Results-Oriented and Relevant, and Time-Bound) goal drafted by the PBIS Tier 2 sub-team based on targeted/at-risk academic data of the students participating in each Tier 2 intervention at the school. This collective Tier 2 Intervention SMART goal is monitored with data at least twice a month by the Tier 2 sub-team.

SMART Goal Behavior: A Tier 2 behavioral goal is a targeted/at-risk intervention behavioral SMART goal drafted by the PBIS Tier 2 sub-team based on targeted/at-risk behavioral data of the students participating in each Tier 2 intervention at the school. This collective Tier 2 Intervention SMART goal is monitored with data at least twice a month by the Tier 2 sub-team.

How to establish a PBIS Champion Model Silver School is outlined in the next chapters. **As you begin this journey, please make sure to continue referring to the critical takeaways of this book:** *Build on the Tier 1 behavior system foundation of your school (addresses approximately 80 percent of students in a tiered behavior system), create a Tier 2 behavior response system with procedures and protocols in place to address targeted/at-risk behavior needs (addresses approximately 10 to 15 percent of students in a tiered behavior system), and develop, audit, and implement a menu of Tier 2 interventions within this Tier 2 system based on student needs and data.*

Part II
The PBIS Tier Two Handbook

Getting Started With Category A— Tier 2 Markers

This chapter identifies and describes the Tier 2 markers of a Silver Level PBIS Champion Model, explains how to assess your system's current state relative to each marker, presents some challenges real schools face and approaches to address those challenges, and provides detailed lists of actions for moving your system toward its desired future—Silver Level PBIS Champion Model. The intent of this chapter is to help you build a system designed to support the effective delivery of Tier 2 interventions at your school.

What is a Tier 2 behavior system? A Tier 2 behavior system at a school is designed to support 10 to 15 percent of the school's population. Typically, Tier 2 interventions are provided to students demonstrating targeted/at-risk behavior needs. The ultimate goal is to help these students before their behavior escalates to the next level of interventions. Often these students need the social skills, strategies, or supports tailored to their social-emotional needs in addition to receiving the school-wide social-emotional supports at the school available for all students. In order to have an effective Tier 2 behavior system, school leaders and their staff need to be able to articulate the Who? What? How? and Measured? for every Tier 2 intervention offered at their school, and there needs to be clear evidence of implementation. This chapter will help you identify any gaps in developing such a system. If you have more than 10 to 15 percent of the students needing Tier 2 interventions at your school, it is highly recommended to revisit your school-wide foundation (See *The PBIS Tier One Handbook*).

CRITICAL TAKEAWAYS

- In this chapter you will learn how to implement the eight markers essential for building a Tier 2 behavior system at your school. Implementing all eight Tier 2 markers with fidelity will help you create an effective and sustainable Tier 2 behavior system designed to support the menu of Tier 2 interventions offered at your school. You will learn how to establish and implement Tier 2 interventions in Chapter 4.
- Without a system to support implementation, monitoring, and communication of the offered Tier 2 interventions at your school, they will not work.
- In this chapter, you will find criteria and examples of evidence for each marker. Please do not get overwhelmed; select one or two actions at a time and make sure they are implemented with fidelity.
- Use a systematic lens of the school as you navigate through each marker in this chapter. The focus is on creating the system. In Chapter 4, the focus will be on what each Tier 2 intervention offered at your school should include in order to be effective for students.

So what are the Tier 2 markers of a Silver Level PBIS Champion Model?

In order to build a strong Tier 2 behavior system, eight critical markers must be in place:

 Marker 1: Establish and Operate an Effective PBIS Tier 2 Sub-Team

 Marker 2: Establish and Maintain Tier 2 Staff Commitment

 Marker 3: Establish a Tier 2 Data-Based Process for Identifying Students

 Marker 4: Establish a Tier 2 Data Entry Procedure and Review Plan

 Marker 5: Establish a Tier 2 Fidelity Check Process

 Marker 6: Develop and Deliver Tier 2 Lesson Plans

 Marker 7: Establish a Tier 2 Behavior Incentive System

 Marker 8: Establish a Tier 2 System for Monitoring and Communicating Progress

Marker 1 icon: iStock.com/appleuzr; Marker 2 icon: iStock.com/Passakorn_14; Marker 3 icon: iStock.com/appleuzr; Marker 4 icon: iStock.com/-VICTOR-; Marker 5 icon: iStock.com/Skarin; Marker 6 icon: iStock.com/appleuzr; Marker 7 icon: iStock.com/tkacchuk; Marker 8 icon: iStock.com/Irena Tsoneva

These eight Tier 2 markers can be assessed through the Tier 2 Markers Scoring Rubric (T2-MSR), a tool used to help a school establish a Tier 2 behavior system implementation baseline and recognized as a valid tool to measure and monitor progress of implementing PBIS Tier 2 markers in schools. A complete T2-MSR can be found at the end of the chapter. The indicator evidencing a strong Tier 2 behavior system foundation in alignment with the Silver PBIS Champion Model is an overall **T2-MSR score of 80 percent or higher, which is equivalent to 39 points or more out of a total 48 points.**

We use the T2-MSR score as one of the measures for evidencing attainment of a Tier 2 PBIS Silver Champion Model. The first step toward developing a Tier 2 Silver Champion Model is to assess the current state of your own system using the T2-MSR. You will use the results of this tool to perform a gap analysis and get an understanding of where your system is in relation to the eight critical Tier 2 markers. It is important that honest responses are provided for all the T2-MSR items, because the information gained from the rubric data is used to guide your next-step actions.

Who should complete the Tier 2 Markers Scoring Rubric (T2-MSR)? To ensure accurate baseline information is collected, a PBIS Tier 2 sub-team should complete the rubric. If you do not have a PBIS Tier 2 sub-team established at the time of the baseline rubric, the administrator of the school should complete the initial rubric in collaboration with his or her school leadership team or other selected stakeholders.

TIER 2: THE EIGHT PBIS TIER 2 MARKERS

This section presents each of the eight Tier 2 PBIS markers, including the following details:

- Description of the marker
- Questions to consider in relation to the marker
- Assessing our current state with the T2-MSR: Where are we in relation to this marker?
- List of actions to advance the marker from current state to desired future and a reflection about next-step, high-leverage moves
- Cautions or red flags indicating that one or more areas of the marker may need to be addressed
- Examples from the field: challenges, practical solutions, and tools/resources to use

LET'S GET STARTED WITH TIER 2 MARKERS

MARKER 1
Establish and Operate an Effective PBIS Tier 2 Sub-Team

Assemble a PBIS Tier 2 sub-team, three to four members from the PBIS school-wide team (e.g., representation from administration, teacher coach, support service provider), who can commit to meeting at least forty-five minutes to an hour twice a month (bi-monthly) to plan, implement, and monitor Tier 2 interventions in the school. An administrator is an active member of this team and guarantees that the team has time to meet and the resources needed to be successful. The PBIS Tier 2 sub-team has a designated lead who helps organize and ensure the meetings are taking place in an organized and consistent fashion, ensures information is being shared at least bi-monthly with the staff that have students participating in a Tier 2 intervention and the broader PBIS team, monthly with the entire staff, and follows up on the commitments the sub-team makes during their bi-monthly meetings, in addition to attending the monthly school-wide PBIS team meetings.

Note

Some schools incorporate their academic and behavior tiered system team meetings together; that is sufficient as long as the Tier 2 behavior system component of the agenda is given the attention needed for successful Tier 2 intervention implementation. It is suggested that the PBIS Tier 2 sub-team meets at least twice a month. It is suggested that the information from the Tier 2 sub-team meeting is shared with the stakeholders and the broader PBIS team at least twice a month. It is suggested the rest of the staff is updated on Tier 2 interventions at least monthly at a staff meeting or other method (e.g., "We currently have 8 students in CICO Tier 2 intervention; 6 are responding and meeting their goals, and 2 are continuing to struggle. We are going to adjust some things with the 2 students and discuss moving them to another intervention as a team if they do not respond to the modifications to their CICO plan").

Questions to Consider

Does our school have a PBIS Tier 2 sub-team? If yes, is our team operating effectively?

_____

_____

_____

Does the membership of our PBIS Tier 2 sub-team include an administrator and staff member with expertise in creating behavior interventions?

_____

_____

_____

_____

Does our PBIS Tier 2 sub-team understand the purpose of their role?

_____

_____

_____

_____

Does our administrator actively support the PBIS Tier 2 sub-team by attending all meetings as well as by supporting the decisions and work of the PBIS Tier 2 sub-team?

_____

_____

_____

_____

Does our PBIS Tier 2 sub-team meet at least bi-monthly for forty-five minutes to an hour?

_____

_____

_____

_____

Assessing Our Current State: Section of the T2-MSR
Where Are We in Relation to Marker 1?

Marker 1: Establish and Operate Effective PBIS Tier 2 Sub-Team

Criteria	2 Points	1 Point	0 Points	Score
PBIS Tier 2 sub-team is assembled	The PBIS Tier 2 sub-team comprises at least 3–4 members from the school-wide PBIS team. The Tier 2 sub-team includes representation from administration and support services. The Tier 2 sub-team meets at least forty-five minutes to an hour at least twice a month (bi-monthly) to plan and monitor Tier 2 intervention implementation and effectiveness.	The PBIS Tier 2 sub-team is established but meetings are held inconsistently and are not a priority.	A PBIS Tier 2 sub-team does not exist at the school.	_____/2
Administrator support is evident	An administrator is an active member of the PBIS Tier 2 sub-team and guarantees that the Tier 2 sub-team has time to meet and the resources.	An administrator is a part of the Tier 2 sub-team but gets pulled away frequently from the meetings.	There is no administrator representation on the Tier 2 sub-team. An administrator does not attend Tier 2 sub-team meetings.	_____/2
PBIS Tier 2 sub-team lead established	The PBIS Tier 2 sub-team has a designated lead. The lead helps organize and ensure the Tier 2 sub-team meetings are taking place and ensures an agenda/checklist is being followed during the meetings.	The Tier 2 sub-team has not yet designated a lead, but an administrator helps facilitate the meetings at this time.	There is no lead established. Meetings are disorganized.	

(Continued)

(Continued)

Criteria	2 Points	1 Point	0 Points	Score
PBIS Tier 2 sub-team lead established (continued)	The lead helps ensure Tier 2 intervention information is being shared at least bi-monthly with the stakeholders and the school-wide PBIS team, and monthly with the rest of the school staff. The lead follows up on the commitments the Tier 2 sub-team makes during their bi-monthly Tier 2 sub-team meetings.	Information from the meetings are not formally documented or shared with the school-wide PBIS team and/ or the school staff.		_____/2
				Total _____6

ACTIONS TO ESTABLISH AND OPERATE AN EFFECTIVE PBIS TIER 2 SUB-TEAM

- The administrator shares the research, purpose, and goals of implementing Tier 2 interventions at the school; their expectations about implementing Tier 2 with fidelity are clear and consistent.
- The administrator can articulate components necessary to establish an effective Tier 2 behavior system.
- The role and purpose of the PBIS Tier 2 sub-team is defined and articulated to the entire school staff.
- All school staff are given the opportunity to be considered as a Tier 2 sub-team member.
- Assemble a PBIS Tier 2 sub-team that includes *at least* three of a diverse representation of staff (from different grade levels, site roles, etc.)—positive, influential members who commit to implementing Tier 2.
- An administrator serves as an active member of the sub-team.
- Ensure at least one member of the PBIS Tier 2 sub-team has expertise in behavior intervention development.

- Calendar bi-monthly PBIS Tier 2 sub-team meetings of at least forty-five minutes to an hour during the duty day or an agreed upon time. The PBIS Tier 2 sub-team must adhere to the meeting schedule.
- The PBIS Tier 2 sub-team members commit to establishing and following an agenda/checklist and norms for each meeting.
- An administrator allows time for the PBIS Tier 2 sub-team lead to organize and prepare for PBIS Tier 2 sub-team meetings. The lead will help facilitate the meetings, monitor the work of the sub-team by ensuring bi-monthly meetings are held, and follows up on commitments made by the PBIS Tier 2 sub-team.
- The PBIS Tier 2 sub-team shares updates (five to ten minutes) with the staff during every staff or department meeting.
- Offer PBIS Tier 2 sub-team membership as an adjunct duty or replacement for supervision duty.
- Provide a stipend to the PBIS sub-team lead.
- Provide an additional preparation period at the secondary level.

CAUTION

If you find one or more of the following conditions or situations occurring at your school, view the condition/situation as a red flag that one or more areas of this marker—Establish and Operate Effective PBIS Tier 2 Sub-Team—may need to be addressed.

RED FLAGS

- The PBIS Tier 2 sub-team has been established but meets for compliance reasons only.
- The PBIS Tier 2 sub-team was thrown together and does not meet regularly to review Tier 2 behavior data.
- The administrator and PBIS Tier 2 sub-team members are unclear as to what it takes to implement an effective Tier 2 behavior system.
- The PBIS Tier 2 sub-team does not include a member with behavior expertise.
- The administrator does not or rarely attends PBIS Tier 2 sub-team meetings.
- The administrator is not supportive, as evidenced by his or her behaviors and actions and by the quality of the decisions and work of the PBIS Tier 2 sub-team.

(Continued)

(Continued)

- No evidence exists of an agenda, checklists, data, norms, and/or actions taken for each team meeting.
- PBIS Tier 2 sub-team meetings are cancelled because other meetings take priority.
- PBIS Tier 2 sub-team meetings are scheduled during non-duty times, and/or PBIS Tier 2 sub-team members are assigned supervision duty or other responsibilities that conflict with PBIS Tier 2 sub-team meeting times and no coverage is provided.
- PBIS Tier 2 sub-team meetings are not focused, and messaging to the entire staff about the work is not clear. (*The consequence is that team members begin to drop off the team because the messaging reflects them in a negative light.*)
- The administrator and PBIS Tier 2 sub-team cannot articulate the purpose for Tier 2 interventions and the relationship to student success.
- The PBIS Tier 2 sub-team does not provide updates to the school-wide PBIS team regularly to prevent misconceptions from forming.
- PBIS Tier 2 sub-team members do not believe in the Tier 2 interventions.

Based on our assessment of the current state for this marker and the suggested list of actions and red flags, what should our next move be?

_____

_____

_____

_____

_____

_____

_____

_____

_____

_____

FROM THE FIELD: MARKER 1—ESTABLISH AND OPERATE AN EFFECTIVE PBIS TIER 2 SUB-TEAM

Challenge: The PBIS Tier 2 sub-team does not have a consistent understanding of how to conduct productive PBIS Tier 2 sub-team meetings. The PBIS Tier 2 sub-team does not have a person designated as the lead to help organize the Tier 2 data and facilitate the sub-team meetings with relevant data. The Tier 2 sub-team members are resistant when asked if they were interested in volunteering as the lead, because they do not feel they will be provided the time needed to effectively prepare for Tier 2 sub-team meetings.

How would you address this challenge?

_____

_____

_____

_____

_____

_____

_____

_____

_____

Practical solution: The administrator decides to make the role of the PBIS Tier 2 sub-team lead an adjunct duty. The administrator provided coverage and/or compensation for the lead to prepare for the bi-monthly sub-team meetings. In addition, the PBIS Tier 2 sub-team developed a checklist of items to utilize as a reference guide at each meeting to ensure the actions they decided were being implemented by their designated timelines.

Tool/resource used: PBIS Tier 2 Sub-Team Meeting Checklist

What is it? It is a tool to assist the PBIS Tier 2 sub-team in covering critical Tier 2 components during their PBIS Tier 2 sub-team meetings. It is also a helpful resource to ensure the Tier 2 sub-team stays on track and logs next step actions and timelines.

PBIS Tier 2 Sub-Team Meeting Checklist	Who	What	When
• Tier 2 sub-team lead reviews the meeting agenda items (ensures sub-team stays on topic).			
• Meeting starts and ends on time (items have time limits that are followed).			
• Check-in on previous meeting next steps. (How did we do?)			
• Meeting minutes are recorded.			
• Review Tier 2 markers.			
• Review Tier 2 characteristics.			
• Review Tier 2 SMART goals.			
• Review Tier 2 intervention data/reports.			
• Discuss progress of students in current Tier 2 interventions.			
• Discuss next steps for students who are not responding to the Tier 2 interventions.			
• Review fidelity of implementation data of the Tier 2 interventions.			
• Discuss incentives provided for students in Tier 2 interventions.			
• Discuss exit plan for students who have met their goals.			
• Review new referrals for Tier 2 interventions and place students appropriately.			
• Discuss follow-up and communication methods with the stakeholders.			
• Develop next steps and assign members their role and an expected completion date.			
• Set follow-up meeting date (new items are added to the next meeting agenda).			
• Other			
• Other			
• Other			

MARKER 2
Establish and Maintain Tier 2 Staff Commitment

Establishing and maintaining Tier 2 staff commitment means that at least 80 percent of the school staff understand, support, and buy into the implementation of the Tier 2 behavior system. Staff directly involved with the offered Tier 2 interventions are updated on the effectiveness of the developed and implemented Tier 2 interventions on at least a bimonthly basis. Staff is provided adequate training on an ongoing basis to build their capacity in articulating and supporting effective Tier 2 implementation. Staff input on how the procedures and processes are working for students receiving Tier 2 interventions is solicited and considered by the Tier 2 sub-team on at least a monthly basis. Staff misconceptions and areas of concerns are addressed in a timely manner.

Questions to Consider

Are data regarding Tier 2 student behavior shared bi-monthly with staff directly involved with the offered Tier 2 interventions?

_____

_____

_____

Does our staff provide input in establishing Tier 2 intervention implementation?

_____

_____

_____

Are staff given ongoing opportunities to provide feedback, offer suggestions, and make decisions regarding Tier 2 intervention implementation?

_____

_____

_____

(Continued)

(Continued)

Is majority approval of staff sought for every Tier 2 intervention implemented, and are only the interventions with majority staff approval implemented?

_____

_____

_____

❧ ❧

Assessing Our Current State: Section of the T2-MSR Where Are We in Relation to Marker 2?

Marker 2: Establish and Maintain Tier 2 Staff Commitment

Criteria	2 Points	1 Point	0 Points	Score
Establish staff commitment	At least 80 percent of the school staff understand, support, and buy into Tier 2 implementation.	At least 50 percent of the school staff understand and support Tier 2 implementation.	The majority of the staff do not understand or support Tier 2 implementation.	_____/2
Maintain staff commitment	Ongoing training and support are provided to staff on Tier 2 implementation.	Minimal ongoing training is provided to the staff on Tier 2 implementation.	No training and support are provided to staff on Tier 2 implementation.	_____/2
Staff input	Staff input on Tier 2 implementation is gathered and considered on at least a bi-monthly basis. Staff is provided updates on at least a bi-monthly basis on the effectiveness of Tier 2 implementation.	Staff input is gathered inconsistently or not considered.	Staff input is not gathered.	_____/2
				Total _____/6

> ### ACTIONS TO ESTABLISH AND
> ### MAINTAIN TIER 2 STAFF COMMITMENT
>
> - Create the need for PBIS Tier 2 implementation.
> - Provide staff with an overview of the research that supports Tier 2 implementation.
> - Provide ongoing training that supports Tier 2 implementation.
> - Designate a portion of each staff or department meeting agenda for teachers to receive updates on Tier 2 implementation and effectiveness.
> - Invite students receiving Tier 2 interventions to share with staff the positive impact the intervention has had on them.
> - Share school behavior data during staff or department meetings and have staff identify areas of need while allowing them to give input.
> - Enlist an influential PBIS Tier 2 sub-team member to share the importance of Tier 2 implementation with the staff.
> - Clarify misconceptions about Tier 2 implementation.
> - Create ongoing opportunities for faculty to provide feedback, offer suggestions, and make decisions regarding PBIS Tier 2 processes. Create a method for staff to provide ongoing input to the PBIS Tier 2 sub-team regarding Tier 2 intervention implementation (i.e., an input board located in a specific room in the school or online).
> - Share Tier 2 intervention behavior data with the entire staff at least monthly and at least twice a month with staff directly involved with the offered Tier 2 interventions.
> - Clearly communicate and message all PBIS Tier 2 information in a timely fashion.
> - Educate staff on the procedures and protocols for referring students for Tier 2 interventions.
> - Revisit the importance of Tier 1 classroom management strategies.
> - Revisit differences in major/minor behavior referrals.
> - Provide clear and timely communication to staff requesting Tier 2 intervention support.
> - Ensure the role of the teacher in the Tier 2 intervention is clear, practical, and consistent.

CAUTION

If you find one or more of the following conditions or situations occurring at your school, view the condition/situation as a red flag that one or more areas of this marker—Establish and Maintain Tier 2 Staff Commitment— may need to be addressed.

RED FLAGS

- The message sent to staff is that Tier 2 implementation replaces discipline.
- Staff are directed to help implement Tier 2 interventions but do not know what it entails.
- Staff input and feedback about Tier 2 interventions and goal setting are not collected and/or used.
- Tier 2 sub-team members serve for compliance reasons only and **do not** believe that Tier 2 implementation will help improve their school's system nor that it is useful as an improvement strategy.
- Staff do not understand their role in the Tier 2 implementation.
- There is a misconception about Tier 2 implementation.
- Tier 2 data are not shared with staff.
- Staff do not understand the purpose of Tier 2 implementation.
- Staff view Tier 2 implementation as optional.
- Staff are not fulfilling Tier 2 intervention obligations.
- Staff do not follow through with the Tier 2 interventions.
- Class time is interrupted without receiving feedback on the best timeslots agreed upon by the stakeholders.

Based on our assessment of the current state for this marker and the suggested list of actions and red flags, what should our next move be?

_____

_____

_____

_____

_____

_____

_____

_____

_____

FROM THE FIELD: MARKER 2—ESTABLISH AND MAINTAIN TIER 2 STAFF COMMITMENT

Challenge: Influential teachers at the school do not think Tier 2 implementation will help students who are demonstrating at-risk behaviors. These particular teachers are familiar only with one Tier 2 intervention that has been inconsistently offered and implemented to students at their school for years. According to their perception, this particular Tier 2 intervention has been ineffective.

How would you address this challenge?

_____

_____

_____

_____

_____

_____

_____

_____

_____

_____

Practical solution: The PBIS Tier 2 sub-team identified that the staff was unclear about the various factors that affect successful Tier 2 implementation. The Tier 2 sub-team wanted a non-threatening way to share the successes of Tier 2 interventions with the staff based on behavior data and student input. In order to do so, they designated a slot on every staff and/or department agenda to provide Tier 2 implementation share-out opportunities. The Tier 2 sub-team developed a simple script to follow as they highlighted success stories. In this case, the PBIS Tier 2 sub-team also invited a student receiving this Tier 2 intervention to share out and describe the positive impact of the intervention to the entire staff.

Tool/resource used: Tier 2 Intervention Success Share-Out Script

What is it? Script to share out Tier 2 intervention successes at staff or department meetings

TIER 2 Intervention
Success Share-Out Script

Description of student's behavior prior to starting the Tier 2 intervention:
Jason was asked to leave class on a daily basis for blurting out and joking throughout the day during instruction.

Description of the Tier 2 intervention student received:
Teacher/student contract intervention with social skills lessons once a week for eight weeks to help him learn how to use replacement behaviors instead of blurting out jokes to receive negative peer attention. The teacher worked in partnership with the school counselor to ensure the appropriate skills were targeted during sessions.

Behavior and academic successes since the intervention:
Jason has improved his grades to a C average. Jason has not been asked to leave the classroom for blurting out in four weeks.

Evidence of success from the Tier 2 intervention:
Jason will present to the staff on how his newly learned skills have helped him meet his Tier 2 intervention goals.

Questions/input process activity steps:

In table groups

- Develop three questions to help clarify or provide additional information regarding this particular Tier 2 intervention share-out topic.
- Develop one suggestion on how to improve Tier 2 implementation.
- Be prepared to share out questions and suggestions to improve Tier 2 implementation.

MARKER 3
Establish a Tier 2 Data-Based Process for Identifying Students

The PBIS Tier 2 sub-team establishes a Tier 2 data-based process for identifying students who need Tier 2 interventions. The PBIS Tier 2 sub-team establishes criteria for enrolling and exiting students from implemented Tier 2 interventions. The PBIS Tier 2 sub-team meets bi-monthly to identify students, review data, and ensure students who are in need of specific Tier 2 interventions are placed in a timely fashion.

Questions to Consider

Has our PBIS Tier 2 sub-team established clear, written procedures that outline the process for responding to students who need additional behavior interventions?

_____

_____

_____

Does a procedure exist in our system to document and track (i.e., a form, database entry, file, or binder) students receiving Tier 2 interventions?

_____

_____

_____

Does written documentation exist in our system that includes all available Tier 2 interventions and clear definitions of what they consist of and how they are accessed?

_____

_____

_____

(Continued)

(Continued)

Is there a set of criteria for each Tier 2 intervention available at the school?

_____

_____

_____

Are all staff members clear about which Tier 2 interventions are appropriate for students displaying a need for additional interventions?

_____

_____

_____

What are our system's predetermined appropriate responses to students needing additional targeted support?

_____

_____

_____

Is there evidence the majority of staff are aware of and use the Tier 2 intervention referral process when needing additional support with a student in need of a Tier 2 intervention?

_____

_____

_____

Assessing Our Current State: Section of the T2-MSR Where Are We in Relation to Marker 3?

Marker 3: Establish a Tier 2 Data-Based Process for Identifying Students

Criteria	2 Points	1 Point	0 Points	Score
Data-based process	The PBIS Tier 2 sub-team has an established data-based process for identifying students in need of Tier 2 interventions.	Behavior data are collected inconsistently and are not used for placing students in Tier 2 interventions.	No data-based process exists for identifying students in need of Tier 2 interventions.	_____/2

Criteria	2 Points	1 Point	0 Points	Score
Established criteria	The PBIS Tier 2 sub-team has established criteria for enrolling and exiting students from Tier 2 interventions. The staff is educated on the criteria for each Tier 2 intervention available at the school.	There are entrance criteria for Tier 2 interventions but no exit criteria. The PBIS Tier 2 sub-team inconsistently uses the Tier 2 intervention criteria for placing students.	No criteria exist for Tier 2 interventions.	_____/2
Review process	The PBIS Tier 2 sub-team meets at least bi-monthly and uses behavior data and Tier 2 intervention referral process to identify, review, and ensure students in need of specific Tier 2 interventions are placed in a timely fashion.	The PBIS Tier 2 sub-team meets at least bi-monthly but does not use data to make decisions about placing or exiting students from Tier 2 interventions.	The PBIS Tier 2 sub-team does not meet to review behavior data. No Tier 2 intervention referral process exists.	_____/2
				Total _____/6

ACTIONS TO ESTABLISH A TIER 2 DATA-BASED PROCESS FOR IDENTIFYING STUDENTS

- Use behavior data to identify what Tier 2 interventions are needed at the school (e.g., Hands Off Academy was developed based on data demonstrating students were having difficulty keeping their hands to themselves).
- Meet as a PBIS Tier 2 sub-team as planned on a bi-monthly basis.
- Develop a Tier 2 intervention referral process that is simple and clear.
- Ensure the majority of staff understand the entrance and exit criteria for each Tier 2 intervention offered at the school.
- Communicate in a timely fashion with stakeholders who are asking for additional supports.
- Attain feedback from all stakeholders prior to placing students in Tier 2 interventions.
- Ensure exit criteria are monitored and communicated to all stakeholders.
- Communicate the student's progress with stakeholders on a regular basis.
- Advocate for the needed Tier 2 interventions at the school based on behavior data.
- Ensure the administrator is an active member of this process.

CAUTION

If you find one or more of the following conditions or situations occurring at your school, view the condition/situation as a red flag that one or more areas of this marker—Establish a Tier 2 Data-Based Process for Identifying Students—may need to be addressed.

RED FLAGS
• Too many students needing Tier 2 interventions (over 15 to 20 percent of the school population). • Weak Tier 1 foundation. • Tier 2 interventions offered do not match the need of the student(s) based on behavior data. • Tier 2 interventions are not offered in a timely fashion. • No criteria exist for getting students into or exited from the Tier 2 • interventions. • Staff are unaware of the referral process and/or student placement into a Tier 2 intervention. • Tier 2 interventions do not include an instructional component (i.e., specific behaviors are not explicitly taught to the student). • There is a misconception that the Tier 2 interventions are full. • Not enough supports and/or human capital allocated for Tier 2 implementation. • Referring staff are unaware of their role in the Tier 2 intervention process. • Time-consuming rating sheets are provided to staff without buy-in and/or explanation on how to use or interpret their meaning • Staff speak negatively about Tier 2 interventions in the staff lounge.

Based on our assessment of the current state for this marker and the suggested list of actions and red flags, what should our next move be?

_____

_____

_____

_____

FROM THE FIELD: MARKER 3—ESTABLISH A TIER 2 DATA-BASED PROCESS FOR IDENTIFYING STUDENTS

Challenge: A Tier 2 sub-team was doing a good job collecting Tier 1 behavior data from the school but did not have a system in place to identify students in need of additional targeted behavior interventions. The teachers at the school complained about not having any additional interventions available to support students demonstrating at-risk behavior problems.

How would you address this challenge?

_____

_____

_____

_____

_____

_____

_____

_____

_____

_____

    Practical solution: The Tier 2 sub-team created a practical resource for the staff describing each Tier 2 intervention offered at the school while including a detailed explanation of entrance and exit criteria.

    Tool/resource used: Tier 2 Intervention Description and Criteria Reference Sheet

    What is it? The Tier 2 Intervention Description and Criteria Reference Sheet is a resource that summarizes the offered interventions and describes the criteria needed for a student to receive each intervention. This is a great resource for both the PBIS Tier 2 sub-team as well as the entire staff to reference when in need of additional supports for students.

Tier 2 Intervention Description and Criteria Reference Sheet

Name of the Tier 2 Intervention	Description of the Tier 2 Intervention	Criteria for Entry Into the Tier 2 Intervention
Social Skills	Students are taught appropriate social skills and provided opportunities to generalize the newly learned skills in appropriate settings.	• If a student is demonstrating challenges getting along with peers inside and out of the classroom setting • If a student has 3 or more minor referrals • Teacher or administrator referral • Other (e.g., parent request)
Check-In Check-Out (CICO)	Students will be provided with additional positive adult interactions throughout the day to help monitor and give feedback on appropriate behaviors. Students will be taught the skills they need to meet their CICO goals.	• If a student is demonstrating repeated challenges of following rules in the classroom setting • If a student has 3 or more minor classroom referrals • Teacher or administrator referral • Other (e.g., parent request, support services request)
Hands Off Academy	Students will be provided instruction on how to keep their hands to themselves. They will be taught how to assess their anger triggers and have the opportunities to practice appropriate replacement behaviors.	• If a student is demonstrating challenges keeping their hands to themselves. • If a student has 3 minor physical contact referrals or has a major physical contact referral/incident • Teacher or administrator referral • Other (e.g., parent request, support provider request)
Behavior Contract	Students will work with an adult to develop and monitor a behavior contract. They will be taught how to meet the requirements on the behavior contract.	• If a student is demonstrating challenges with a specific behavior (e.g., tardiness to class, lack of homework completion) • If a student has 3 or more incidents of the same addressed behavior • Teacher or administrator referral • Other (e.g., parent request)
Class Break	Students will be taught strategies to calm down when they perceive an unfair situation in the classroom setting. They will be taught how to use a class break process and use their newly learned skills to calm down and return back to class without their behaviors escalating.	• If a student is demonstrating challenges calming down when upset • If a student has 3 or more minor referrals or major referral resulting from escalation of behavior when upset • Teacher or administrator referral • Other (e.g., parent request, support provider request)

Extra Resource: Tier 2 Supports At-A-Glance	
Tier 2 Supports At-A-Glance	
Total number of students enrolled at the school.	
How many Tier 2 interventions are available for students on your campus? List names of the interventions.	
How many students are receiving Tier 2 interventions on your campus?	
Percentage of students receiving Tier 2 interventions at your school. (Total number of students receiving Tier 2 interventions divided by total number of students enrolled at the school = % of students on a Tier 2 intervention)	

Note

No more than 10 to 15 percent of students at the school should be receiving a Tier 2 intervention. If you receive a higher percentage, it is suggested you revisit your Tier 1 system.

Tier 2 Supports: Student Data Drill Down					
Student Name	**Grade**	**Tier 2 Intervention Name**	**Reason the Student Needs the Tier 2 Intervention**	**Do All Stakeholders Know Their Role With the Tier 2 Intervention?**	**Next Steps**

MARKER 4
Establish a Tier 2 Data Entry Procedure and Review Plan

The PBIS Tier 2 sub-team establishes a Tier 2 data entry procedure and review plan to ensure accurate and up-to-date Tier 2 intervention data are analyzed, communicated to, and understood by the PBIS sub-team, stakeholders, and staff. A Tier 2 data entry procedure is the process of inputting Tier 2 behavior data into an information management system equipped with the capabilities to produce behavior reports, graphs, and charts for the Tier 2 PBIS sub-team for use in problem-solving and decision-making (Note: Other data collection methods are also acceptable for monitoring purposes, such as Google Sheets, Excel, or other preferred tracking sheets or programs). A Tier 2 data review plan is designed to help monitor progress toward meeting PBIS Tier 2 intervention academic and behavior SMART goals and inform the system about the effectiveness of Tier 2 intervention implementation.

❧❧

Questions to Consider

Does our school have a process for collecting behavior data to identify and monitor effectiveness of programs students receive during targeted Tier 2 interventions?

_____

_____

_____

Does our school have a person identified who ensures the data are being collected and inputted regularly (Tier 2 collected data is up-to-date by the end of each week)?

_____

_____

_____

Does our PBIS sub-team review the data as a team and share student progress with stakeholders on at least a bi-monthly basis in a format that is easy to understand?

_____

_____

_____

❧❧

Assessing Our Current State: Section of the T2-MSR Where Are We in Relation to Marker 4?

Marker 4: Establish a Tier 2 Data Entry Procedure and Review Plan

Criteria	2 Points	1 Point	0 Points	Score
Data entry procedures	Clear and consistent data entry procedures are in place for the collection and inputting of Tier 2 intervention data. Data entry procedures are implemented with fidelity, and the Tier 2 intervention data are up-to-date prior to every Tier 2 sub-team meeting. There is a designated PBIS Tier 2 sub-team member who helps ensure Tier 2 intervention data procedures are being followed with fidelity.	Data entry procedures for entering Tier 2 intervention data are inconsistent. The Tier 2 intervention data are not up-to-date. No one has been designated to monitor Tier 2 intervention data entry procedures.	No procedures exist to collect and enter Tier 2 intervention data.	_____/2
Data management system	There is a Tier 2 intervention data management system equipped with the capabilities to produce behavior reports, graphs, and/or charts for the Tier 2 sub-team to use for problem-solving and decision-making. (*Note:* This may include but is not limited to data collection methods such as Google sheets, Excel, SWIS/CICO online monitoring system or other tracking sheets/programs).	No formal system exists for Tier 2 intervention data management. The Tier 2 sub-team informally collects Tier 2 intervention data; the data are presented in a disorganized fashion.	No Tier 2 intervention data management system exists.	_____/2
Review plan	The PBIS Tier 2 sub-team has established a Tier 2 intervention review plan to ensure accurate and up-to-date Tier 2 intervention	The PBIS Tier 2 sub-team does not have a formal Tier 2 review plan.	No plan exists to analyze Tier 2 intervention	

(Continued)

(Continued)

Criteria	2 Points	1 Point	0 Points	Score
Review plan (continued)	data are analyzed, communicated to, and understood by the PBIS sub-team, stakeholders, and the school-wide PBIS team (bi-monthly basis).	Areas of Tier 2 interventions that are not working are discussed, but not regularly nor in an organized fashion using data to problem solve.	data for effectiveness.	_____/2
				Total _____/6

**ACTIONS TO ESTABLISH A TIER 2
DATA ENTRY PROCEDURE AND REVIEW PLAN**

- Designate a staff member to input Tier 2 behavior data in chosen monitoring system.
- Train staff members on the Tier 2 data collection procedures and processes.
- Develop a flowchart for staff to reference as they collect Tier 2 intervention data.
- Make data collection practical and easy to use for staff.
- Administrator ensures Tier 2 data are updated at least twice a month (best practice is to have Tier 2 intervention data by the end of each week).
- Provide a stipend, if available, to a staff member to input the Tier 2 intervention data.
- Update the PBIS wall in the staff lounge or online in a shared format with Tier 2 intervention progress graphs.
- Provide staff with updates regarding Tier 2 intervention effectiveness.
- Provide Tier 2 intervention data collection booster sessions.
- Administrator ensures Tier 2 data reports are prepared for the PBIS Tier 2 meetings.
- Ensure data collected matches the Tier 2 intervention SMART goals.
- Provide time or coverage for the designated data person to ensure data are being collected correctly.

CAUTION

If you find one or more of the following conditions or situations occurring at your school, view the condition/situation as a red flag that one or more areas of this marker—Establish a Tier 2 Data Entry Procedure and Review Plan—may need to be addressed.

RED FLAGS
• No procedures exist to collect Tier 2 intervention data.
• Tier 2 intervention data are not updated prior to Tier 2 sub-team meetings.
• No methods exist for monitoring students receiving Tier 2 interventions.
• The administrator does not provide time for the designated data entry person to organize the Tier 2 intervention data.
• No systems or methods exist to track Tier 2 data or create charts/graphs to visually demonstrate student progress.
• Collected data are not shared with staff in a manner that is easy to understand.
• Staff are unclear on how to fill out the data forms connected with Tier 2 interventions.
• Tier 2 intervention decisions are made without the use of data.

Based on our assessment of the current state for this marker and the suggested list of actions and red flags, what should our next move be?

_____

_____

_____

_____

_____

_____

_____

_____

_____

_____

_____

FROM THE FIELD: MARKER 4—
ESTABLISH A TIER 2 DATA ENTRY
PROCEDURE AND REVIEW PLAN

Challenge: The PBIS Tier 2 sub-team met bi-monthly to discuss Tier 2 implementation but lacked a process to review collected Tier 2 intervention data and use it for problem-solving.

How would you address this challenge?

_____

_____

_____

_____

_____

_____

_____

_____

_____

_____

_____

Practical solution: The PBIS Tier 2 sub-team created a shared Google sheet for inputting and monitoring Tier 2 intervention data on an ongoing basis. They designated a member of the Tier 2 sub-team to ensure the Tier 2 intervention progress monitoring form was updated prior to every Tier 2 sub-team meeting.

Tool/resource used: Template for Tier 2 Intervention Monitoring

What is it? The Template for Tier 2 Intervention Monitoring is designed to help PBIS Tier 2 sub-teams monitor and discuss Tier 2 intervention student progress for every PBIS Tier 2 intervention offered at their school. Reviewing and discussing progress of students utilizing this template is part of every Tier 2 sub-team meeting as a fixed agenda item.

Template for Tier 2 Intervention Monitoring

Bi-monthly Progress Review Date	Student Name	Tier 2 Intervention	# of Minor Behavior Referrals	# of Major Behavior Referrals	Meeting Tier 2 Intervention Goals Academics and Behavior	Suspension Days	Continue Intervention, Change Intervention, or Exit Intervention	Other Identified Actions
Example: March 13— Reviewing data from February 27–March 13	Fred	Check-In Check-Out (starting date February 27, 2017)	2 minor disruptions in class	0 majors	Academics— yes Behavior—yes	0 suspensions	Continue intervention	Adjust Check-In Check-Out goal

Note

Each student receiving a Tier 2 intervention at your school should be monitored in this format or a similar format at each Tier 2 sub-team meeting.

MARKER 5
Establish Tier 2 Fidelity Check Process

The PBIS Tier 2 sub-team establishes a Tier 2 fidelity check process to ensure Tier 2 interventions are being implemented with fidelity. Fidelity of implementation is evaluated at multiple levels (e.g., administration, stakeholder/staff, student, and parent/guardian). The PBIS Tier 2 sub-team helps ensure all stakeholders/staff are implementing their role in the Tier 2 intervention with fidelity by frequent check-ins, observations, and opportunities for the staff/stakeholders to provide input and suggestions and request additional supports.

Questions to Consider

Does a method exist for our Tier 2 sub-team to monitor the fidelity of Tier 2 intervention implementation?

_____

_____

(Continued)

Marker 5 icon: iStock.com/Skarin

(Continued)

_____

Are Tier 2 intervention fidelity data reviewed by the Tier 2 sub-team at least bi-monthly?

_____

_____

_____

Does a process exist to improve Tier 2 implementation fidelity based on the fidelity data collected and analyzed by the Tier 2 sub-team?

_____

_____

_____

Are staff trained to help them better address Tier 2 implementation fidelity?

_____

_____

_____

Assessing Our Current State: Section of the T2-MSR Where Are We in Relation to Marker 5?

Marker 5: Establish Tier 2 Fidelity Check Process

Criteria	2 Points	1 Point	0 Points	Score
Fidelity check process	The PBIS Tier 2 sub-team established a fidelity check process to ensure Tier 2 interventions are being implemented with fidelity.	The PBIS Tier 2 sub-team is in the process of developing a fidelity check process for Tier 2 interventions.	No fidelity check process exists for Tier 2 interventions.	_____/2

Criteria	2 Points	1 Point	0 Points	Score
Multiple levels	Fidelity of implementation is evaluated at multiple levels (e.g., administration, stakeholder/staff, student, and parent/guardian).	Fidelity of Tier 2 implementation is evaluated only by the administration at this time.	Fidelity of Tier 2 implementation is not evaluated at multiple levels.	_____/2
Staff fidelity	About 80% of the staff has bought into implementing their role in Tier 2 interventions with fidelity. The PBIS Tier 2 sub-team helps ensure the staff/stakeholders are implementing the Tier 2 interventions with fidelity by frequent check-ins and observations and by creating ongoing opportunities to gather feedback and provide additional supports and trainings.	About 50% of the staff has bought into implementing their role in Tier 2 interventions with fidelity. There is no method in place to ensure Tier 2 interventions are being implemented with fidelity by staff.	Majority of the staff do not believe in the implementation of Tier 2 interventions.	_____/2
				Total _____/6

ACTIONS TO ESTABLISH TIER 2 FIDELITY CHECK PROCESS

- Develop a process to monitor Tier 2 intervention implementation at least bi-monthly as a PBIS Tier 2 sub-team (e.g., weekly fidelity check-in form).
- Include monitoring fidelity of Tier 2 interventions as an agenda item during Tier 2 sub-team meetings.

(Continued)

(Continued)

- Educate staff on the fidelity of Tier 2 intervention implementation and provide ongoing training and support as needed throughout the year on a case-by-case basis.
- Send reminders to staff about implementing Tier 2 interventions with fidelity.
- Have one-on-one meetings with staff who need additional support in regard to the implementation of Tier 2 interventions.
- Gain administrator assistance working with resistant staff members.
- Build buy-in during staff meetings (e.g., educate staff on the importance of implementing Tier 2 interventions with fidelity).
- Ensure Tier 2 intervention implementation is clear, consistent, and practical for staff.
- Provide staff feedback on implementation and help follow up with other stakeholders (e.g., parent/guardian).
- Solicit feedback from the students receiving Tier 2 interventions.

CAUTION

If you find one or more of the following conditions or situations occurring at your school, view the condition/situation as a red flag that one or more areas of this marker—Establish Tier 2 Fidelity Check Process—may need to be addressed.

RED FLAGS

- Staff do not believe in implementing Tier 2 interventions.
- Staff do not follow through with the Tier 2 intervention implementation.
- Communication on student progress is nonexistent.
- Students do not understand their role in the Tier 2 intervention.
- Staff do not understand their role in the Tier 2 intervention.
- Progress of SMART goals are not reviewed with the students or communicated to the stakeholders.
- Tier 2 interventions are not delivered consistently.
- No positive outcomes have come about as a result of Tier 2 interventions not being implemented with fidelity.
- Incentives for Tier 2 interventions are not provided consistently for students meeting their SMART goals.
- No procedures exist to continue a Tier 2 intervention when a staff member is absent.

❧❧

Based on our assessment of the current state for this marker and the suggested list of actions and red flags, what should our next move be?

_____

_____

_____

_____

_____

_____

_____

_____

❧❧

FROM THE FIELD: MARKER 5—ESTABLISH TIER 2 FIDELITY CHECK PROCESS

Challenge: The PBIS Tier 2 sub-team did not have a method to ensure the Tier 2 interventions were being implemented with fidelity. No method existed to check in with staff/stakeholders to review the adult role in whether or not the Tier 2 intervention was effective.

❧❧

How would you address this challenge?

_____

_____

_____

_____

_____

(Continued)

(Continued)

_____

_____

_____

_____

_____

❧❦❧

Practical solution: The Tier 2 sub-team developed the Tier 2 Intervention Fidelity Check Form, which was completed based on the input from stakeholders in each Tier 2 intervention at the school. The designated Tier 2 sub-team member provided a hard copy or emailed the staff/stakeholders involved in the Tier 2 intervention every Friday. Gathering this fidelity data helped the Tier 2 sub-team address any areas that need improvement for the Tier 2 intervention to be effective.

Tool/resource used: Tier 2 Intervention Fidelity Check Form

What is it? The Tier 2 Intervention Fidelity Check Form is designed to monitor the fidelity of Tier 2 intervention implementation and identify areas within the Tier 2 intervention that need refining. The PBIS Tier 2 sub-team reviews this information bi-monthly and makes modifications or suggestions to improve Tier 2 implementation based on the collected fidelity feedback.

Note

In this example, stakeholder feedback was collected once a week and reviewed at least twice a month by the Tier 2 sub-team. Some schools also collect feedback via email check ins on Fridays or other online methods.

Student name:				
Tier 2 intervention name:				
Teacher/staff name:				
Date:				

Tier 2 Intervention Fidelity Check Form

S = Student	T = Teacher	P = Parent	A = Administrator

Week (date)	Did we follow the Tier 2 intervention with fidelity?				If no, what can we do to improve implementation?
	S	T	P	A	
Monday					
Tuesday					
Wednesday					
Thursday					
Friday					

MARKER 6
Develop and Deliver Tier 2 Lesson Plans

Develop Tier 2 lesson plans to teach students skills and strategies during Tier 2 intervention sessions. Deliver behavior lessons in a small-group or individualized fashion, whichever method is best for the student. Use a variety of teaching strategies and/or methods that will help students generalize their newly learned skills. Behavior lessons need to include strategies to help students meet their Tier 2 academic and behavior SMART goals. Students should receive 30- to 45-minute weekly sessions targeting their needed skills over the course of at least six to eight weeks.

Note

A bonus set of lessons aligned with the Tier 2 Intervention: Hands Off Academy is provided for you after Chapter 4 as a reference.

Questions to Consider

Does your school have an instructional component to the Tier 2 interventions offered?

_____

_____

_____

Does your school have a bank of behavior lessons aligned to each Tier 2 intervention offered?

_____

_____

_____

Are the behavior lessons provided with fidelity to the students receiving Tier 2 interventions?

_____

_____

_____

Does your school have a process to help students generalize their learned skills in the appropriate settings?

_____

_____

_____

Are SMART goals set with students receiving Tier 2 interventions, both academic and behavioral?

_____

_____

_____

Assessing Our Current State: Section of the T2-MSR Where Are We in Relation to Marker 6?

Marker 6: Develop and Deliver Tier 2 Lesson Plans

Criteria	2 Points	1 Point	0 Points	Score
Lesson plans	The PBIS Tier 2 sub-team has organized, developed, and arranged designated staff to deliver lessons aligned to each Tier 2 intervention at the school.	The PBIS Tier 2 sub-team has organized and developed Tier 2 intervention lessons but have not been able to identify staff to deliver the lessons.	The PBIS Tier 2 sub-team has not organized, developed, or delivered Tier 2 lessons.	

(Continued)

(Continued)

Criteria	2 Points	1 Point	0 Points	Score
Lesson plans (continued)	The administrator has ensured that staff in charge of delivering the Tier 2 intervention lessons have the time and support to do so consistently.			_____/2
Delivery	Behavior lessons are delivered in small-group or individualized settings using a variety of teaching strategies and methods to help students generalize learned skills. Behavior lessons are delivered consistently. Tier 2 intervention lessons include strategies to help students meet their Tier 2 intervention SMART goals.	Behavior lessons are delivered in small-group or individualized settings but do not include a variety of teaching strategies and/or methods to help students generalize. Behavior lessons are delivered inconsistently; often the sessions are cancelled because of other priorities.	Behavior lessons are not delivered in any fashion.	_____/2
Duration	Students receive 30–45 minutes of a Tier 2 intervention behavior lesson at least once a week based on their needed skills and progress. Tier 2 intervention behavior lessons are delivered for at least six to eight weeks.	Students receive 30–45 minutes of a Tier 2 intervention behavior lesson at least once a week over the course of six to eight weeks. Tier 2 intervention behavior lessons are not aligned to each Tier 2 intervention.	Students do not receive 30–45 minutes of a Tier 2 intervention behavior lesson in any fashion.	_____/2
				Total _____/6

ACTIONS TO DEVELOP AND DELIVER TIER 2 LESSON PLANS

- Ensure each Tier 2 intervention behavior lesson addresses the function of the behavior (*Notes:* Utilize student support services staff to help identify the reason or function of the at-risk behavior. Common functions include but are not limited to: Escape, Tangible, Attention Seeking, Sensory, Lack of Social Skills).
- Develop, find, or purchase lessons online that are developmentally appropriate for students in each Tier 2 intervention. (See pbisworld.com or pbischampionmodelsystem.com for lesson resources.)
- Administrator allows and creates an environment for the teaching of behavior lessons for students receiving Tier 2 interventions.
- Connect the Tier 2 behavior lessons back to the behavior expectations of the school and the function of the students' behaviors.
- Provide students receiving Tier 2 intervention behavior lessons opportunities to practice their newly learned skills in the appropriate settings (e.g., role play, observation and practice of learned skills, homework assignments, challenges).
- Focus on one or two skills at a time during behavior lessons.
- Revisit and review learned skills with the students.
- Utilize multiple methods and strategies for delivering behavior lessons.
- Allow students to provide feedback in what would be helpful for them during behavior lessons.
- Provide one-on-one lessons for students who are having difficulty in a group setting.
- Seek input from staff on the best lesson delivery time options.
- Follow up with stakeholders on suggestions and progress of the students.
- Provide a description of Tier 2 interventions in the school or district handbook.
- Allow students to help establish lessons and projects.
- Have a lesson makeup plan in place.

CAUTION

If you find one or more of the conditions or situations listed on the next page occurring at your school, view the condition/situation as a red flag that one or more areas of this marker—Develop and Deliver Tier 2 Lesson Plans—may need to be addressed.

RED FLAGS

- Tier 2 interventions do not include a teaching component.
- Behavior lessons are not aligned with the goals of the Tier 2 intervention.
- Limited resources are available for staff delivering Tier 2 interventions.
- Students do not receive at least six to eight sessions to learn new skills and strategies.
- The function of the student's behavior is not identified.
- Replacement behaviors are not taught to the students.
- SMART goals are unattainable.
- Staff expectation of progress is unrealistic (i.e., overnight success).
- Staff delivering Tier 2 behavior lessons do not believe the students can benefit from the behavior lessons.
- Staff use Tier 2 interventions as another "we did one more thing that didn't work" with regard to the documentation toward removing a student from the school.
- Staff do not implement the behavior lessons with fidelity.
- Staff cancel behavior lessons.
- Staff pull students out of class at inconsistent times without collaborating with the stakeholders.
- Staff do not communicate with stakeholders on progress.
- Staff do not provide a real-life practice component for the students to generalize what they've learned.
- Administrators ignore the challenges staff are facing with the Tier 2 intervention implementation (e.g., student not attending).
- Administrators do not place students in an appropriate Tier 2 intervention in a timely manner.
- Staff use the most common Tier 2 intervention at the school for every situation.
- Staff does not feel comfortable to ask for help if a student is not responding to the lessons.

Based on our assessment of the current state for this marker and the suggested list of actions and red flags, what should our next move be?

_____

_____

_____

_____

_____

_____

_____

_____

❧❧

FROM THE FIELD: MARKER 6—DEVELOP AND DELIVER TIER 2 LESSON PLANS

Challenge: The PBIS Tier 2 sub-team was having difficulty developing or finding behavior lessons for each of the designated Tier 2 interventions offered at the school. Although each teacher had a social-emotional behavior kit of lessons in their classroom as part of the school's Tier 1 school-wide implementation of behavior skills, the Tier 2 sub-team did not feel the same resources were appropriate for students identified to receive specific targeted/at-risk interventions. In addition, their support services provider was at their school only one day a week, so they wanted to organize Tier 2 intervention behavior lesson topics with multiple strategies to fit their needs with the resources they have.

❧❧

How would you address this challenge?

_____

_____

_____

_____

_____

_____

(Continued)

(Continued)

_____

_____

_____

❧❧❧

Practical solution: The Tier 2 sub-team worked with the behavior specialist on their Tier 2 sub-team to create a template called the Tier 2 Intervention/Behavior Academy Planning Guide to organize the lessons, skills, and strategies to be taught in each of the sessions. Their intent was to prepare a frame of lessons and resources for staff delivering Tier 2 behavior lessons for reference as needed for each Tier 2 intervention offered. This helped them save time by having materials and resources organized using this template.

Tool/resource used: Tier 2 Intervention/Behavior Academy Planning Guide

What is it? This is a guide and accountability sheet to ensure students receiving Tier 2 interventions are receiving behavior lessons designed to meet their needs.

Tier 2 Intervention/Behavior Academy Planning Guide
Name of the intervention/behavior academy: Social Skills Academy: Listening **Description/purpose of the intervention/behavior academy:** The purpose of this Tier 2 intervention is to help students learn the skills needed to listen to their teachers in the classroom setting. **Criteria to enter the intervention/behavior academy:** On average, two to three minor referrals for noncompliance a week.
Criteria to exit the intervention/behavior academy: Actively engaging in at least six to eight sessions of social skills academy and meeting academic and behavior SMART goals by the end of eight weeks. Student will continue if he/she needs additional supports to help them meet their goals before exiting from the Tier 2 intervention. In addition, all stakeholder input is considered before the student exits from the Tier 2 intervention. **Overall goal/outcome(s) from the intervention/behavior academy:** On average: zero to one minor referral for noncompliance a week and making progress in reading benchmark standards.

Sample Sessions:

Extra Resource: Function of Behavior Cheat Sheet

Session	Outcome of the Session	Behavior Lesson or Activity/ Exercise Needed	Measure
Session 1	Interview and goal setting with the students	Interview student https://www.pbis.org/ resource/352/classroom-student-interview-use-for-functional-assessment Introduce listening skills https://powertochange.com/ students/people/listen/	Verbalize, write down, or model three of the learned listening skills
Session 2	Introduce listening skill steps	Red Light Green Light http://www.boystowntraining. org/assets/	Verbalize and generalize listening skill steps
Session 3	Practice listening and following directions skill steps	Listen and Drawing Activities http://www.bbc.co.uk/skillswise/ worksheet/en34type-e1-w-listen-and-draw	Follow skill steps
Session 4	Explain listening skill steps and provide examples of how they are used in the class setting	Create listening skill poster and practice presenting	Explain skill steps correctly as they present their posters

Note

Please work with a support services provider (e.g., school psychologist) or behavior expert to help identify the function of student behavior in order to provide a relevant intervention.

Extra Resource: Function of Behavior Checklist	
Common Functions of Student Behavior . . .	**Justify why you believe the student is demonstrating or not demonstrating each of these functions.**
Escape: Student is escaping from a task or activity he/she does not want to engage in.	
Tangible: Student is demonstrating a desire for a specific item or activity.	
Attention seeking: Student is desiring attention from peers and/or adults.	
Sensory: Student is engaging in behavior that feels good and meets his/her sensory needs.	
Lack of social skills: Student does not have the social skills necessary to demonstrate proper behavior.	

MARKER 7
Establish a Tier 2 Incentive System

Establish a Tier 2 incentive system designed to provide incentives to students meeting their Tier 2 intervention SMART goals. Obtain student and staff feedback when designing and selecting appropriate incentives. Ensure there are allocated funds for the purchase and delivery of Tier 2 incentives in a timely and consistent fashion. At least 80 percent of the staff understand the reasons for establishing a Tier 2 incentive system and have bought into the implementation.

Questions to Consider

Does our school have a system for providing meaningful incentives to students who are meeting their Tier 2 intervention SMART goals?

_____

_____

_____

Marker 7 icon: iStock.com/tkacchuk

Do we consistently provide students with incentives for meeting their SMART goals?

_____

_____

_____

Do we survey the students to see what incentives they would like to receive for meeting their SMART goals?

_____

_____

_____

Does our school allocate funds or have other ways of ensuring incentives can be purchased and provided for students?

_____

_____

_____

Does a procedure exist in the event that the person distributing incentives is off campus or unavailable?

_____

_____

_____

Assessing Our Current State: Section of the T2-MSR Where Are We in Relation to Marker 7?

Marker 7: Establish a Tier 2 Incentive System

Criteria	2 Points	1 Point	0 Points	Score
Incentive system	There is an established system that provides incentives to students for making progress toward or attaining their Tier 2 intervention academic and behavior SMART goals. There are a variety of Tier 2 intervention incentives available for students based on student feedback. Adequate funding is allocated for Tier 2 intervention incentive opportunities. Staff input on incentives is considered. At least 80% of the staff understands the reasons to establish a Tier 2 system and have bought into the process.	The school-wide PBIS incentives are in place, but there is no clear system for Tier 2 intervention incentives. The PBIS Tier 2 sub-team is in the process of developing Tier 2 intervention incentives but has not surveyed the students or staff on preferences. At least 50% of the staff continues to feel that students receiving Tier 2 interventions should not receive any incentives.	A Tier 2 incentive system is not in place at the school. Majority of the staff do not agree that students receiving Tier 2 interventions should receive incentives.	_____/2
Aligned with Tier 2 intervention SMART goals	The Tier 2 intervention system is designed to reward students who are making progress or attaining their Tier 2 intervention SMART academic and behavior goals. *Note:* There needs to be a clear outline and instruction to the students on how incentives are earned.	The Tier 2 incentives system is beginning to be developed. The Tier 2 sub-team is working on developing clear procedures for aligning Tier 2 incentives and student SMART goals.	There is no alignment with the Tier 2 incentives and student SMART goals at this time.	_____/2

Criteria	2 Points	1 Point	0 Points	Score
Consistent and meaningful	Tier 2 incentives are consistently given to students for meeting their SMART goals (at least once a week). Feedback from students is gathered and taken into consideration as the Tier 2 incentives are being purchased and designed. Students find the Tier 2 incentives to be meaningful.	Tier 2 incentives are not consistently given to students meeting their SMART goals (at least once a week). Feedback from students is not considered as the Tier 2 sub-team designs incentives. Students do not find the incentives to be meaningful.	Tier 2 incentives are nonexistent.	_____/2
				Total _____/6

ACTIONS TO ESTABLISH A TIER 2 INCENTIVE SYSTEM

- Survey students to see what incentives are meaningful for them.
- Establish SMART goals for students receiving Tier 2 interventions with stakeholder input. (See Chapter 5.)
- Make sure the SMART goals are attainable so the students feel success.
- Create a consistent time to distribute Tier 2 incentives.
- Stay consistent with incentives.
- Educate staff on the importance of Tier 2 incentives.
- Survey staff on their perceptions of Tier 2 incentives.
- Make sure the timing of incentive distribution is agreed upon (e.g., some teachers do not want Tier 2 incentives given to students in front of the entire class; they prefer students be released a few minutes early Friday afternoon to receive their incentive by the designated person).
- Allocate adequate funding to support Tier 2 incentives.
- Solicit community resources and/or stores for donations.
- Understand the funding sources in your school and/or district; request to align a social-emotional school goal with a funding source.
- Designate a staff member to help with incentive distribution.

CAUTION

If you find one or more of the following conditions or situations occurring at your school, view the condition/situation as a red flag that one or more areas of this marker—Establish a Tier 2 Incentive System—may need to be addressed.

RED FLAGS

- Adults decide what incentives the students will like.
- Students receiving Tier 2 interventions are not surveyed on what they would like to work toward earning.
- The designated staff member forgets to award the Tier 2 incentives on at least a weekly basis.
- Teachers are frustrated with students being given incentives for "behaving the way they are supposed to."
- Data are not up-to-date; therefore, staff doesn't know if a student earned their incentive.
- Procedures do not exist for when the staff designated to distribute Tier 2 incentives is off campus or unavailable.
- Tier 2 incentives are not available for students.

Based on our assessment of the current state for this marker and the suggested list of actions and red flags, what should our next move be?

_____

_____

_____

_____

_____

_____

_____

_____

_____

FROM THE FIELD: MARKER 7— ESTABLISH A TIER 2 INCENTIVE SYSTEM

Challenge: Several Tier 2 interventions are offered to students demonstrating at-risk behaviors. However, the school does not have a process for surveying students on what they would like to work toward for meeting Tier 2 intervention SMART goals. The Tier 2 incentives currently offered are not motivational for the students and do not involve a timeline for delivery.

How would you address this challenge?

_____

_____

_____

_____

_____

_____

_____

_____

_____

Practical solution: The PBIS Tier 2 sub-team designed a brief student survey to help staff develop reasonable and attainable incentives based on student input.

Tool/resource used: Tier 2 Intervention Incentive Survey

What is it? This is a brief survey designed to help Tier 2 sub-team members obtain insight into student preferences for incentives. This survey is also utilized with students at the beginning of a Tier 2 intervention. Students are made aware of their SMART goal incentive timelines and what they need to meet their goals.

Student name:	
Tier 2 intervention:	
Interviewer name:	
Tier 2 Incentive Student Survey	**Responses and Notes**
1. Why are you receiving this Tier 2 intervention?	
2. Do you know why you are having challenges with this behavior (e.g., avoiding work, feeling angry)?	
3. What do you hope to learn from this Tier 2 intervention?	
4. What are your intervention SMART goals?	
5. What is something you would like to work toward or earn every week?	
6. Do you prefer free time? If so, what would you like to do on your free time?	
7. How do you earn this selected incentive?	
8. When is the incentive given to you?	
9. What is the plan if you do not meet your daily or weekly goals?	
10. How do you ask for help if you are not meeting your goals?	

MARKER 8
Establish a Tier 2 System for Monitoring and Communicating Progress

The PBIS Tier 2 sub-team establishes a system for monitoring and communicating Tier 2 intervention progress with all stakeholders. Students receiving Tier 2 interventions will be monitored on a daily, weekly, and bi-monthly basis depending on the Tier 2 intervention and their SMART goals. A variety of communication methods will be utilized to share progress data with the students, staff/stakeholders,  and parents/guardians. A process exists to modify and communicate changes to the Tier 2 interventions based on progress data with all stakeholders.

Marker 8 icon: iStock.com/Irena Tsoneva

Questions to Consider

Does our school have a system to monitor Tier 2 intervention progress?

_____

_____

_____

Does our school have a system to communicate Tier 2 intervention progress?

_____

_____

_____

Do we consistently provide Tier 2 intervention feedback to all stakeholders?

_____

_____

_____

Do we consistently solicit Tier 2 intervention progress input from all stakeholders?

_____

_____

_____

Does our school have a system for communicating Tier 2 progress to the parents or guardians of the student?

_____

_____

_____

(Continued)

(Continued)

Does our school have a process to adjust and modify Tier 2 interventions based on progress data?

_____

_____

_____

❧❧❧

Assessing Our Current State: Section of the T2-MSR Where Are We in Relation to Marker 8?

Marker 8: Establish a Tier 2 System for Monitoring and Communicating Progress

Criteria	2 Points	1 Point	0 Points	Score
System for monitoring	There is a system for monitoring Tier 2 intervention progress for every Tier 2 intervention offered at the school. Students receiving Tier 2 interventions are monitored on a daily, weekly, and bi-monthly basis, depending on the Tier 2 intervention they are receiving.	Students receiving Tier 2 interventions are inconsistently monitored.	No system exists for monitoring Tier 2 intervention progress.	_____ /2
System for communication	There is a system for communicating Tier 2 intervention progress with all stakeholders on at least a weekly basis.	Tier 2 intervention progress is informally and inconsistently communicated with all stakeholders.	No system exists for communicating Tier 2 intervention progress with all stakeholders.	

(Continued)

Criteria	2 Points	1 Point	0 Points	Score
System for communication (continued)	A variety of communication methods are utilized to communicate Tier 2 intervention progress data (e.g., phone call, email, notes home, meetings, etc.). The system allows for reciprocal communication amongst stakeholders. *Note:* Stakeholders may include but are not limited to staff, support service provider, administrator, PBIS Tier 2 sub-team lead, and parent/guardian.	At least half of the stakeholders involved with the Tier 2 intervention are informed of Tier 2 intervention progress on a weekly basis.		_____/2
Plan for modifying and communicating changes with Tier 2 Interventions	There is a plan for modifying and communicating Tier 2 intervention changes with all stakeholders based on collected progress data and stakeholder feedback.	There is a plan for modifying Tier 2 intervention changes based on data. Changes are inconsistently communicated with all stakeholders.	No plan exists for modifying and communicating Tier 2 intervention changes with all stakeholders based on data.	_____/2
				Total _____/6

ACTIONS TO ESTABLISH A TIER 2 SYSTEM FOR MONITORING AND COMMUNICATING PROGRESS

- Develop a data monitoring form or process aligned with the collective SMART goals and incentive plan for each Tier 2 intervention offered at the school.
- Ensure the data monitoring form or process gathers data aligned with the Tier 2 intervention goals.

(Continued)

(Continued)

- Decide on a preferred method of communication with stakeholders on at least a weekly basis.
- Decide on a preferred method of communication with staff involved with the Tier 2 intervention on at least a weekly basis.
- Set check-in times with all stakeholders implementing the Tier 2 interventions (calendar them to ensure they take place).
- Educate all stakeholders on the importance of monitoring and working in collaboration.
- Establish a system for communication when a student is not responding to the Tier 2 intervention as planned.
- Establish criteria for whether the Tier 2 intervention needs to be stopped or continued with modifications (e.g., 6–8 weeks).
- Identify a surrogate at the school to help monitor the Tier 2 intervention if the parent or guardian is not consistently returning communication.

Note

Best practice is to work with the family if possible.

CAUTION

If you find one or more of the following conditions or situations occurring at your school, view the condition/situation as a red flag that one or more areas of this marker—Establish a Tier 2 System for Monitoring and Communicating Progress—may need to be addressed.

RED FLAGS

- The PBIS Tier 2 sub-team stops monitoring the Tier 2 intervention data consistently.
- The PBIS Tier 2 sub-team becomes complacent in their Tier 2 intervention monitoring and communication procedures.
- The Tier 2 intervention goals are unclear and difficult to monitor.
- The Tier 2 intervention goals are not aligned with the Tier 2 interventions.

- The PBIS Tier 2 sub-team does not communicate progress of the Tier 2 intervention to all stakeholders on a regular basis (at least weekly).
- The PBIS Tier 2 sub-team does not have a variety of methods for communication with all stakeholders; they use the same method for all stakeholders even if the stakeholders are not responding.
- Stakeholders are not aware of how to provide feedback about the Tier 2 interventions.
- No Tier 2 intervention training exists for the stakeholders to become educated on monitoring and communication procedures.
- The PBIS Tier 2 sub-team does not communicate with stakeholders who did not receive Tier 2 intervention data.
- Communication only takes place when the Tier 2 intervention is not working instead of consistently throughout the intervention.
- The majority of the stakeholders do not believe in the Tier 2 intervention; they are participating only at a compliance level.

Based on our assessment of the current state for this marker and the suggested list of actions and red flags, what should our next move be?

_____

_____

_____

_____

_____

_____

_____

_____

_____

_____

FROM THE FIELD: MARKER 8—ESTABLISH A SYSTEM FOR MONITORING AND COMMUNICATING TIER 2 INTERVENTION PROGRESS WITH STAKEHOLDERS

Challenge: A handful of students were meeting their behavior Tier 2 Intervention CICO goals (e.g., not blurting out in class); however, they were not completing any academic work in class. The teachers were frustrated because they felt that the students were being rewarded for their naughty behaviors.

❧❧❧

How would address this challenge?

_____

_____

_____

_____

_____

_____

_____

_____

_____

❧❧❧

Practical solution: The administrator, with the help of the Tier 2 PBIS sub-team, created a student academic monitoring sheet to help the teacher monitor the Tier 2 academic goals in a practical way. This form was completed and reviewed with the stakeholders on a weekly basis.

Tool/resource used: CICO Student Academic Goal Monitoring Sheet

What is it? This monitoring sheet is one example an administrator used that helped teachers support CICO students who were not completing academic work. In this case, the administrator met with the teacher and student to discuss the collected data on this form for a month. This helped with accountability and a collaborative approach for this Tier 2 intervention.

Student name _____

Starting date _____

Classroom teacher _____

CICO intervention teacher/staff: _____

CICO Student Academic Goal Monitoring Sheet

Homework goal: 75% of homework will be completed weekly.

Classwork goal: 75% of classwork will be completed weekly.

Weekly rating scale:

0 (50% work left incomplete)

1 (75% of work completed)

Week of _____	Homework goal progress (How am I doing?) 0 or 1	Classwork goal progress (How am I doing?) 0 or 1	Additional notes:
Week of _____	Homework goal progress (How am I doing?) 0 or 1	Classwork goal progress (How am I doing?) 0 or 1	Additional notes:
Week of _____	Homework goal progress (How am I doing?) 0 or 1	Classwork goal progress (How am I doing?) 0 or 1	Additional notes:
Week of _____	Homework goal progress (How am I doing?) 0 or 1	Classwork goal progress (How am I doing?) 0 or 1	Additional notes:
End of 4 week totals:	Homework total: ____/4 = _____%	Classwork total: ____/4 = _____%	Total of both homework and classwork:____/8 = _____%

Tier 2 Markers Scoring Rubric (T2-MSR) Full Version

Criteria	2 Points	1 Point	0 Points	Score
Marker 1: Establish and Operate Effective PBIS Tier 2 Sub-Team				
PBIS Tier 2 sub-team is assembled	The PBIS Tier 2 sub-team comprises at least 3–4 members from the school-wide PBIS team. The Tier 2 sub-team includes representation from administration and support services. The Tier 2 sub-team meets at least forty-five minutes to an hour at least twice a month (bi-monthly) to plan and monitor Tier 2 intervention implementation and effectiveness.	The PBIS Tier 2 sub-team is established but meetings are held inconsistently and are not a priority.	A PBIS Tier 2 sub-team does not exist at the school.	_____/2
Administrator support is evident	An administrator is an active member of the PBIS Tier 2 sub-team and guarantees that the Tier 2 sub-team has time to meet and the resources.	An administrator is a part of the Tier 2 sub-team but gets pulled away frequently from the meetings.	There is no administrator representation on the Tier 2 sub-team. An administrator does not attend Tier 2 sub-team meetings.	_____/2
PBIS Tier 2 sub-team lead established	The PBIS Tier 2 sub-team has a designated lead. The lead helps organize and ensure the Tier 2 sub-team meetings are taking place and ensures an agenda/ checklist is being followed during the meetings.	The Tier 2 sub-team has not yet designated a lead, but an administrator helps facilitate the meetings at this time.	There is no lead established. Meetings are disorganized.	

Criteria	2 Points	1 Point	0 Points	Score
PBIS Tier 2 sub-team lead established (continued)	The lead helps ensure Tier 2 intervention information is being shared at least bi-monthly with the stakeholders and the school-wide PBIS team, and monthly with the rest of the school staff. The lead follows up on the commitments the Tier 2 sub-team makes during their bi-monthly Tier 2 sub-team meetings.	Information from the meetings are not formally documented or shared with the school-wide PBIS team and/or the school staff.		_____/2
				Marker 1 Total ___/6
Marker 2: Establish and Maintain Tier 2 Staff Commitment				
Establish staff commitment	At least 80 percent of the school staff understand, support, and buy into Tier 2 implementation.	At least 50 percent of the school staff understand and support Tier 2 implementation.	The majority of the staff do not understand or support Tier 2 implementation.	_____/2
Maintain staff commitment	Ongoing training and support are provided to staff on Tier 2 implementation.	Minimal ongoing training is provided to the staff on Tier 2 implementation.	No training and support are provided to staff on Tier 2 implementation.	_____/2
Staff input	Staff input on Tier 2 implementation is gathered and considered on at least a bi-monthly basis. Staff is provided updates on at least a bi-monthly basis on the effectiveness of Tier 2 implementation.	Staff input is gathered inconsistently or not considered.	Staff input is not gathered.	_____/2
				Marker 2 Total ___/6

(Continued)

(Continued)

Criteria	2 Points	1 Point	0 Points	Score
Marker 3: Establish a Tier 2 Data-Based Process for Identifying Students				
Data-based process	The PBIS Tier 2 sub-team has an established data-based process for identifying students in need of Tier 2 interventions.	Behavior data are collected inconsistently and are not used for placing students in Tier 2 interventions.	No data-based process exists for identifying students in need of Tier 2 interventions.	_____/2
Established criteria	The PBIS Tier 2 sub-team has established criteria for enrolling and exiting students from Tier 2 interventions. The staff is educated on the criteria for each Tier 2 intervention available at the school.	There are entrance criteria for Tier 2 interventions but no exit criteria. The PBIS Tier 2 sub-team inconsistently uses the Tier 2 intervention criteria for placing students.	No criteria exist for Tier 2 interventions.	_____/2
Review process	The PBIS Tier 2 sub-team meets at least bi-monthly and uses behavior data and Tier 2 intervention referral process to identify, review, and ensure students in need of specific Tier 2 interventions are placed in a timely fashion.	The PBIS Tier 2 sub-team meets at least bi-monthly but does not use data to make decisions about placing or exiting students from Tier 2 interventions.	The PBIS Tier 2 sub-team does not meet to review behavior data. No Tier 2 intervention referral process exists.	_____/2
				Marker 3 Total ___/6
Marker 4: Establish a Tier 2 Data Entry Procedure and Review Plan				
Data entry procedures	Clear and consistent data entry procedures are in place for the collection and inputting of Tier 2 intervention data. Data entry procedures are implemented with fidelity, and the Tier 2 intervention data are up-to-date prior to every Tier 2 sub-team meeting.	Data entry procedures for entering Tier 2 intervention data are inconsistent. The Tier 2 intervention data are not up-to-date.	No procedures exist to collect and enter Tier 2 intervention data.	

Criteria	2 Points	1 Point	0 Points	Score
Data entry procedures (continued)	There is a designated PBIS Tier 2 sub-team member who helps ensure Tier 2 intervention data procedures are being followed with fidelity.	No one has been designated to monitor Tier 2 intervention data entry procedures.		_____/2
Data management system	There is a Tier 2 intervention data management system equipped with the capabilities to produce behavior reports, graphs, and/or charts for the Tier 2 sub-team to use for problem-solving and decision-making. (*Note:* This may include but is not limited to data collection methods such as Google sheets, Excel, SWIS/CICO online monitoring system or other tracking sheets/programs).	No formal system exists for Tier 2 intervention data management. The Tier 2 sub-team informally collects Tier 2 intervention data; the data are presented in a disorganized fashion.	No Tier 2 intervention data management system exists.	_____/2
Review plan	The PBIS Tier 2 sub-team has established a Tier 2 intervention review plan to ensure accurate and up-to-date Tier 2 intervention data are analyzed, communicated to, and understood by the PBIS sub-team, stakeholders, and the school-wide PBIS team (bi-monthly basis).	The PBIS Tier 2 sub-team does not have a formal Tier 2 review plan. Areas of Tier 2 interventions that are not working are discussed, but not regularly nor in an organized fashion using data to problem solve.	No plan exists to analyze Tier 2 intervention data for effectiveness.	_____/2
				Marker 4 Total ___/6

(Continued)

(Continued)

Criteria	2 Points	1 Point	0 Points	Score
Marker 5: Establish Tier 2 Fidelity Check Process				
Fidelity check process	The PBIS Tier 2 sub-team established a fidelity check process to ensure Tier 2 interventions are being implemented with fidelity.	The PBIS Tier 2 sub-team is in the process of developing a fidelity check process for Tier 2 interventions.	No fidelity check process exists for Tier 2 interventions.	_____/2
Multiple levels	Fidelity of implementation is evaluated at multiple levels (e.g., administration, stakeholder/staff, student, and parent/guardian).	Fidelity of Tier 2 implementation is evaluated only by the administration at this time.	Fidelity of Tier 2 implementation is not evaluated at multiple levels.	_____/2
Staff fidelity	About 80% of the staff has bought into implementing their role in Tier 2 interventions with fidelity. The PBIS Tier 2 sub-team helps ensure the staff/stakeholders are implementing the Tier 2 interventions with fidelity by frequent check-ins and observations and by creating ongoing opportunities to gather feedback and provide additional supports and trainings.	About 50% of the staff has bought into implementing their role in Tier 2 interventions with fidelity. There is no method in place to ensure Tier 2 interventions are being implemented with fidelity by staff.	Majority of the staff do not believe in the implementation of Tier 2 interventions.	_____/2
				Marker 5 Total ___/6

Criteria	2 Points	1 Point	0 Points	Score
Marker 6: Develop and Deliver Tier 2 Lesson Plans				
Lesson plans	The PBIS Tier 2 sub-team has organized, developed, and arranged designated staff to deliver lessons aligned to each Tier 2 intervention at the school. The administrator has ensured that staff in charge of delivering the Tier 2 intervention lessons have the time and support to do so consistently.	The PBIS Tier 2 sub-team has organized and developed Tier 2 intervention lessons but have not been able to identify staff to deliver the lessons.	The PBIS Tier 2 sub-team has not organized, developed, or delivered Tier 2 lessons.	____/2
Delivery	Behavior lessons are delivered in small-group or individualized settings using a variety of teaching strategies and methods to help students generalize learned skills. Behavior lessons are delivered consistently. Tier 2 intervention lessons include strategies to help students meet their Tier 2 intervention SMART goals.	Behavior lessons are delivered in small-group or individualized settings but do not include a variety of teaching strategies and/or methods to help students generalize. Behavior lessons are delivered inconsistently; often the sessions are cancelled because of other priorities.	Behavior lessons are not delivered in any fashion.	____/2

(Continued)

(Continued)

Criteria	2 Points	1 Point	0 Points	Score
Duration	Students receive 30–45 minutes of a Tier 2 intervention behavior lesson at least once a week based on their needed skills and progress. Tier 2 intervention behavior lessons are delivered for at least six to eight weeks.	Students receive 30–45 minutes of a Tier 2 intervention behavior lesson at least once a week over the course of six to eight weeks. Tier 2 intervention behavior lessons are not aligned to each Tier 2 intervention.	Students do not receive 30–45 minutes of a Tier 2 intervention behavior lesson in any fashion.	_____/2
				Marker 6 Total ___/6
Marker 7: Establish a Tier 2 Incentive System				
Incentive system	There is an established system that provides incentives to students for making progress toward or attaining their Tier 2 intervention academic and behavior SMART goals. There are a variety of Tier 2 intervention incentives available for students based on student feedback. Adequate funding is allocated for Tier 2 intervention incentive opportunities. Staff input on incentives is considered. At least 80% of the staff understands the reasons to establish a Tier 2 system and have bought into the process.	The school-wide PBIS incentives are in place, but there is no clear system for Tier 2 intervention incentives. The PBIS Tier 2 sub-team is in the process of developing Tier 2 intervention incentives but has not surveyed the students or staff on preferences. At least 50% of the staff continues to feel that students receiving Tier 2 interventions should not receive any incentives.	A Tier 2 incentive system is not in place at the school. Majority of the staff do not agree that students receiving Tier 2 interventions should receive incentives.	_____/2

Criteria	2 Points	1 Point	0 Points	Score
Aligned with Tier 2 intervention SMART goals	The Tier 2 intervention system is designed to reward students who are making progress or attaining their Tier 2 intervention SMART academic and behavior goals. *Note:* There needs to be a clear outline and instruction to the students on how incentives are earned.	The Tier 2 incentives system is beginning to be developed. The Tier 2 sub-team is working on developing clear procedures for aligning Tier 2 incentives and student SMART goals.	There is no alignment with the Tier 2 incentives and student SMART goals at this time.	_____/2
Consistent and meaningful	Tier 2 incentives are consistently given to students for meeting their SMART goals (at least once a week). Feedback from students is gathered and taken into consideration as the Tier 2 incentives are being purchased and designed. Students find the Tier 2 incentives to be meaningful.	Tier 2 incentives are not consistently given to students meeting their SMART goals (at least once a week). Feedback from students is not considered as the Tier 2 sub-team designs incentives. Students do not find the incentives to be meaningful.	Tier 2 incentives are nonexistent.	_____/2
				Marker 7 Total ___/6

(Continued)

(Continued)

Criteria	2 Points	1 Point	0 Points	Score
Marker 8: Establish a Tier 2 System for Monitoring and Communicating Progress				
System for monitoring	There is a system for monitoring Tier 2 intervention progress for every Tier 2 intervention offered at the school. Students receiving Tier 2 interventions are monitored on a daily, weekly, and bi-monthly basis, depending on the Tier 2 intervention they are receiving.	Students receiving Tier 2 interventions are inconsistently monitored.	No system exists for monitoring Tier 2 intervention progress.	_____/2
System for communication	There is a system for communicating Tier 2 intervention progress with all stakeholders on at least a weekly basis. A variety of communication methods are utilized to communicate Tier 2 intervention progress data (e.g., phone call, email, notes home, meetings, etc.). The system allows for reciprocal communication amongst stakeholders. *Note:* Stakeholders may include but are not limited to staff, support service provider, administrator, PBIS Tier 2 sub-team lead, and parent/guardian.	Tier 2 intervention progress is informally and inconsistently communicated with all stakeholders. At least half of the stakeholders involved with the Tier 2 intervention are informed of Tier 2 intervention progress on a weekly basis.	No system exists for communicating Tier 2 intervention progress with all stakeholders.	_____/2

Criteria	2 Points	1 Point	0 Points	Score
Plan for modifying and communicating changes with Tier 2 Interventions	There is a plan for modifying and communicating Tier 2 intervention changes with all stakeholders based on collected progress data and stakeholder feedback.	There is a plan for modifying Tier 2 intervention changes based on data. Changes are inconsistently communicated with all stakeholders.	No plan exists for modifying and communicating Tier 2 intervention changes with all stakeholders based on data.	_____/2
				Marker 8 Total ___/6

OVERVIEW OF CATEGORY A
T2-MSR RESULTS: TIER 2 MARKERS

Category A: Tier 2 Markers	
Category A: Scores for Tier 2 markers	**What is your score?**
Marker 1: Establish and Operate an Effective PBIS Tier 2 Sub-Team	_____/6
Marker 2: Establish and Maintain Tier 2 Staff Commitment	_____/6
Marker 3: Establish a Tier 2 Data-Based Process for Identifying Students	_____/6
Marker 4: Establish a Tier 2 Data Entry Procedure and Review Plan	_____/6
Marker 5: Establish Tier 2 Fidelity Check Process	_____/6
Marker 6: Develop and Deliver Tier 2 Lesson Plans	_____/6
Marker 7: Establish a Tier 2 Incentive System	_____/6
Marker 8: Establish a Tier 2 System for Monitoring and Communicating Progress	_____/6
Goal is 80% or higher	Total Score: _____/48 = _____%

What's Next?

Now that you have learned the necessary Tier 2 markers for creating a strong Tier 2 system, you are ready to design and implement a menu of Tier 2 interventions for your Tier 2 system. In the next chapter, you will learn how to audit and refine each offered Tier 2 intervention at your school to include the five characteristics necessary for effectiveness.

Getting Started With Category B— Tier 2 Characteristics

This chapter identifies and describes the five Tier 2 characteristics that need to be present in each Tier 2 intervention offered at your school. The Tier 2 characteristics guide you through an assessment of your current state, present challenges from the field with practical solutions, and prompt reflection based on Tier 2 assessment data about next-step actions to move your system from current state to desired future—Silver PBIS Champion Model. A school functioning at the Silver PBIS Champion Model level will have evidence of these five Tier 2 characteristics for *at least* the most commonly used Tier 2 intervention at the school; however, the ultimate goal is to ensure that *every* Tier 2 intervention offered at your school can demonstrate evidence of these five Tier 2 characteristics as well. Specifically, this chapter is designed to help you develop, implement, audit, and monitor each Tier 2 intervention offered at your school using the five Tier 2 characteristics as a guide.

Figure 4.1 on the next page gives an example of what we mean by a menu of Tier 2 interventions available at a school. In simple terms, it is a method of organizing all the Tier 2 interventions offered at your school. Note: Some schools may only offer one Tier 2 intervention at the beginning

CRITICAL TAKEAWAYS

- In Chapter 3, you began the hard work of building a Tier 2 behavior system designed to support the implementation of effective Tier 2 interventions.
- In this chapter, you will learn how to establish and implement the five characteristics essential for each Tier 2 intervention offered at your school.
- We recommend that any Tier 2 intervention offered at your school needs to include evidence for all five characteristics introduced in this chapter. For example, if you decide to audit your Tier 2 Check-In Check-Out (CICO) intervention or your Social Skills Group Intervention using this chapter as a guide, you will need to ensure that all five characteristics are in place with fidelity for each intervention.
- The five characteristics in this chapter are designed to help you evaluate the level of fidelity in the Tier 2 interventions currently offered at your school and help you establish new or enhance current Tier 2 interventions based on the need and data of your school.
- In the previous chapter, we asked you to view the eight Tier 2 markers from a systems level lens. For the purpose of this chapter, it is important to evaluate each of these five characteristics using a Tier 2 intervention specific lens (e.g., evaluate, enhance, or develop the five characteristics for each Tier 2 intervention offered at your school).

TIP: Utilize school or district-level staff with behavior expertise as you develop, enhance, and refine effective Tier 2 interventions at your school using these five characteristics as a guide.

of this journey; the ultimate goal is that as your Tier 2 system is established, additional Tier 2 interventions will be available for your students based on your school's needs and data.

Figure 4.1

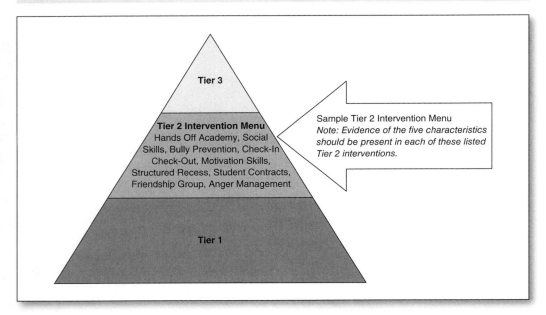

So what are the five Tier 2 characteristics? The five characteristics are as follows:

1. Existence of Criteria and Timely Referral Process

2. Visibility of Tier 2 Intervention Schedule

3. Evidence of Behavior Lessons and Social Skills

4. Existence of Academic/Behavior Goals/Incentives

5. Plan for Progress Monitoring/Communication

Note

The eight Tier 2 markers reviewed in the previous chapter helped us understand the big picture of Tier 2 systems. The five Tier 2 characteristics are designed to help us audit and refine each Tier 2 intervention offered at the school.

TIER 2 CHARACTERISTICS

A strong Tier 2 PBIS system that supports the implementation of effective Tier 2 interventions will have evidence of a strong Tier 1 PBIS foundation firmly in place and all eight Tier 2 markers (Chapter 3) established.

For each Tier 2 intervention offered at your school, you need to ensure each of the five Tier 2 characteristics are present. These five Tier 2 characteristics can best be captured and assessed through the completion of the Tier 2 Intervention Snapshot Interview. (Full version is available at the end of this chapter.)

Note

Conduct a Tier 2 Intervention Snapshot Interview for each Tier 2 intervention offered at your school.

This interview process and tool was designed to gather evidence for Tier 2 intervention implementation through observations and evidence of these characteristics. It provides a snapshot view of each Tier 2 intervention in place at the school based on the input from the implementers, evidence presented, and Tier 2 data. This process of designing, implementing, and collecting evidence for each of these five Tier 2 characteristics should, at minimum, be conducted at the beginning of the year to collect baseline data and again at the end of the year to measure progress, make comparisons, and identify successes or areas for improvement.

Who should complete the Tier 2 Intervention Snapshot Interview?

To obtain accurate baseline information, first look to an external assessor, such as a person from the district office trained in PBIS. If your district does not have an identified person who supports the PBIS work in schools, the site administrator in collaboration with the PBIS coach or school site leadership team should complete this interview. Full version of the Tier 2 Intervention Snapshot Interview is available at the end of this chapter.

How will this interview data be used?

You will use the results of the Tier 2 Intervention Snapshot Interview to perform a gap analysis to gain a better understanding of where each of your Tier 2 interventions are in relation to the five Tier 2 characteristics. You will calculate your points for each of the five characteristics and receive an overall score for each Tier 2 intervention offered at your school.

Note

For the purpose of Silver PBIS Champion Model status, you will need to demonstrate the On Target level with evidence for your most commonly used Tier 2 intervention. However, as mentioned earlier, best practice would be to have all five Tier 2 characteristics in place for each Tier 2 intervention offered at your school.

TIER 2 INTERVENTION SNAPSHOT INTERVIEW SCORING GUIDE

On Target	8-10 points
Making Progress	4-7 points
Needs Improvement	0-3 points

Evidence of a strong Tier 2 intervention is an overall Tier 2 Intervention Snapshot Interview score in the 8 to 10 *On Target* point range. This Tier 2 Intervention Snapshot Interview data should be used as another valuable information stream to inform next steps. Therefore, it is important that objective responses are provided. The results from the Tier 2 Intervention Snapshot Interview is one measure to evidence attainment of a Tier 2 Silver PBIS Champion Model status.

A first step toward developing a Tier 2 Silver PBIS Champion Model school is to assess the current state of your own system, then identify next-step, high-leverage actions based on data analysis, taking into consideration not only data from your Tier 2 Intervention Snapshot Interview but the results of your eight critical Tier 2 marker assessments (Category A—Chapter 3).

The next section of this chapter guides you through a quick assessment of each of the five Tier 2 characteristics, provides you with the opportunity to reflect on the current state and next steps for each Tier 2 intervention at your school, and presents challenges and practical solutions from the field.

Note

See the ends of Chapter 3 and Chapter 4 for full versions of the assessment tools for the Tier 2 markers and Tier 2 characteristics.

TIP: *To begin, go through each of the five characteristics for the most commonly used Tier 2 intervention at your school first.*

Note

In order to provide you with a reference to how this works, the challenges and evidence demonstrating the implementation of the five Tier 2 characteristics will be highlighted for a Tier 2 intervention called Hands Off Academy. Hands Off Academy is a Tier 2 intervention designed to help teach students the social skills needed to keep their hands to themselves and generalize their learned replacement behaviors and strategies in all settings. In addition, at the end of this chapter, you will be provided with a bonus set of Hands Off Academy behavior lessons as an additional resource for your school.

In this section, you will audit your current Tier 2 interventions using the five Tier 2 characteristics as a guide. The items from the Tier 2 Intervention Snapshot Interview are divided into the five characteristics.

TIP: *As you go through each of the five Tier 2 characteristics in this section, identify your most commonly used Tier 2 intervention to begin this process. When your Tier 2 sub-team can demonstrate evidence for each of the five Tier 2 characteristics for your most commonly used Tier 2 intervention at your school, go through this same process with a critical eye for any additional Tier 2 interventions offered at your school. Use this template to help organize which Tier 2 interventions you have audited using this process.*

Tier 2 Intervention Name	C1—In Place or Not in Place	C2—In Place or Not in Place	C3—In Place or Not in Place	C4—In Place or Not in Place	C5—In Place or Not in Place
Most commonly used Tier 2 Intervention:					
Name an additional Tier 2 intervention here:					
Name an additional Tier 2 intervention here:					

C=Characteristic

TIME TO BEGIN: TIER 2 CHARACTERISTICS

Tier 2 Characteristic 1
Existence of Criteria and Timely Referral Process
There are entrance and exit criteria established for this Tier 2 intervention. These established criteria are clearly shared with staff. An easy-to-use referral process for this Tier 2 intervention is in place and at least 80% of staff understand and feel comfortable using it. Students needing this Tier 2 intervention and meeting the criteria are placed in a timely fashion (within a week of referral). Student progress is monitored consistently, and a process is in place to exit students who meet their goals and generalize their learned skills based on the collected data and stakeholder feedback.

ASSESSING OUR CURRENT STATE: WHERE ARE WE IN RELATION TO THIS TIER 2 CHARACTERISTIC?

Section of the Tier 2 Intervention Snapshot Interview

Tier 2 Characteristic	Evidence of Characteristic	Points 0—Not in Place 1—In Progress 2—In Place With Evidence
Characteristic 1: Existence of Criteria and Timely Referral Process	• Entrance and exit criteria are established. • A clear referral process is in place. • At least 80% of staff understand the criteria and referral process. • Students who meet the criteria are placed in a timely fashion (within a week of referral).	Total: _____/2

⚬⚬

What actions should we take to move this Tier 2 intervention closer to target on the Tier 2 characteristic?

_____

_____

_____

_____

⚬⚬

FROM THE FIELD:
TIER 2 CHARACTERISTIC 1

Hands Off Academy Tier 2 Intervention Examples

Challenge: No clear process existed for staff to ask for behavior support with students not responding to Tier 1 management systems. Staff were afraid to ask for help, because they did not want to be perceived as not having control of their students' behaviors. They were also repeatedly told the Tier 2 intervention groups were at full capacity.

❧❧

How would you address this challenge?

_____

_____

_____

_____

_____

_____

_____

_____

_____

❧❧

Practical solution: The PBIS Tier 2 sub-team crafted a Tier 2 Intervention Referral Form that was available in hard copy and electronic format designed to give staff a method for asking for help with student behavior. The PBIS sub-team reviewed the referral forms as they were submitted to the administrator and worked with the referring staff to place the student in the appropriate Tier 2 intervention in a timely fashion.

Tool/resource used: Tier 2 Intervention Referral Form

| TIER 2 |
| Intervention Referral Form |

Student: _____ Date: _____

Teacher: _____ Grade: _____

Student strengths/preferences: _____

Area(s) of concern: _____

Tier 1 strategies I've used to manage behavior: _____

Effectiveness of strategies: _____

Other essential information: _____

Tier 2 Intervention options (*Circle your recommendation*): Hands Off Academy, Check-In Check-Out, Social Skills Groups, Homework Academy (*See description of each Tier 2 intervention in the handbook.*)

For Office Use Only:

Response Date: _____ **By Whom?** _____ **Actions:** _____

Revisit By: _____

Extra tool/resource used: Sample Tier 2 Intervention Permission Slip for Hands Off Academy

NOTE

Permission slips are always good practice and indicate parent/guardian awareness and buy-in; however, if you have a parent/guardian who does not consent to the Hands Off Academy, the recommended approach is to indicate in the district handbook or school handbook that Tier 2 interventions will be utilized as part of the PBIS framework at the school similar to the way additional academic supports are provided for students not responding academically. Discuss your options with your district administration and ultimately work to gain the trust and buy-in from the parents/guardians for the best outcomes.

Hands Off Academy Permission Slip

Student's Name _____

Grade _____

Hands Off Academy Description:

_____

_____

_____

_____

Rationale:

_____

_____

_____

_____

Starting Date _____/_____/_____ Ending Date _____/_____/_____

I give permission for the above-mentioned Hands Off Academy to be implemented.

_____   _____/_____/_____

Parent's/Guardian's Signature   Date

| | **Tier 2 Characteristic 2** | |
| | **Visibility of Tier 2 Intervention Schedule** | |

The schedule for this Tier 2 intervention is clear and consistent (at least weekly) for 6 to 8 weeks. Stakeholder input on the schedule was considered. Stakeholders are given a visual calendar, provided reminders, and know where to access the dates and times in case of any schedule changes. The schedule is posted and updated on the PBIS staff wall under the Tier 2 section. Attendance for this Tier 2 intervention is monitored on a regular basis and communicated based on the schedule.

ASSESSING OUR CURRENT STATE: WHERE ARE WE IN RELATION TO THIS TIER 2 CHARACTERISTIC?

Section of the Tier 2 Intervention Snapshot Interview

Tier 2 Characteristic	Evidence of Characteristic	Points 0—Not in Place 1—In Progress 2—In Place With Evidence
Characteristic 2: Visibility of Tier 2 Intervention Schedule	• An intervention schedule is created and provided to the stakeholders to reference the dates and times of the weekly intervention sessions (6–8 weeks). • The schedule is clear, and there is a process for accessing a copy of the schedule and/or changes to it as needed. • Student attendance is monitored and communicated based on the schedule.	Total: ____/2

What actions should we take to move this Tier 2 intervention closer to target on the Tier 2 characteristic?

_____

_____

_____

_____

_____

_____

(Continued)

(Continued)

_____

_____

_____

_____

❧❧

FROM THE FIELD: TIER 2 CHARACTERISTIC 2

Hands Off Academy Tier 2 Intervention Example

Challenge: No consistent schedule existed to monitor or know when Hands Off Academy was being offered. Student attendance was not monitored or communicated to the stakeholders. Teachers felt frustrated by their students being pulled out of class for Hands Off Academy at inconsistent times. Teachers also complained there was no way to verify when Hands Off Academy was being implemented or cancelled each week.

❧❧

How would you address this challenge?

_____

_____

_____

_____

_____

_____

_____

_____

_____

❧❧

Practical solution: The PBIS Tier 2 sub-team developed the Tier 2 Intervention Schedule/Attendance Sheet to track Hands Off Academy and other Tier 2 interventions offered. This improved the visibility of the schedule and implementation for all stakeholders and strengthened the monitoring of student attendance. This schedule and attendance sheet was accessible to the teachers in a shared online folder so they could reference at any time. The Tier 2 sub-team also monitored student intervention schedules/attendance during bi-monthly sub-team meetings to aid in problem-solving decisions.

Tool/resource used: Tier 2 Intervention Schedule/Attendance Sheet

Tier 2 Intervention Schedule/Attendance Sheet

Student name: Jason

Name of intervention: Hands Off Academy

Month: March/April (6–8 weeks)

Dates: Every Thursday from 1:30–2:00

Date of session	Attendance present (P) or absent (A)	If present, rate engagement during the session (1—not engaged to 5—very engaged)
Session 1: March 2	P	3
Session 2: March 9	P	3
Session 3: March 16	A	NA
Session 4: March 23	A	NA
Session 5: March 30	P-Late	2
Session 6: April 6	A	NA
Session 7: April 13	P	4
Session 8: April 20	A	NA

Continue Hands Off Academy or Exit Hands Off Academy Notes (After 6–8 weeks):

Continue this Tier 2 intervention because of attendance issues. Establish a method for ensuring the student is attending each session.

<table>
<tr><td colspan="2" align="center">Tier 2 Characteristic 3
Evidence of Behavior Lessons and Social Skills</td></tr>
<tr><td colspan="2">Evidence of behavior lessons or social skills development is embedded into this Tier 2 intervention session based on student needs. Students are provided instruction on replacement behaviors and given the opportunity to practice and generalize their newly learned social skills and replacement behaviors in the appropriate settings. Behavior lessons and social skills are delivered in a variety of engaging methods (e.g., lesson plans, books, role playing, videos, online, projects, etc.).</td></tr>
</table>

ASSESSING OUR CURRENT STATE: WHERE ARE WE IN RELATION TO THIS TIER 2 CHARACTERISTIC?

Section of the Tier 2 Intervention Snapshot Interview

Tier 2 Characteristic	Evidence of Characteristic	Points 0—Not in Place 1—In Progress 2—In Place With Evidence
Characteristic 3: Evidence of Behavior Lessons and Social Skills	• Behavior lessons and social skills development are utilized during each session. • Behavior lessons and social skills are delivered in a variety of engaging methods. • Students are given opportunities to practice their newly learned social skills.	Total: _____/2

∛∞∛

What actions should we take to move this Tier 2 intervention to target on the Tier 2 characteristic?

_____

_____

_____

_____

_____

_____

_____

_____

_____

_____

❧❧

FROM THE FIELD: TIER 2 CHARACTERISTIC 3

Hands Off Academy Tier 2 Intervention Example

Challenge: Hands Off Academy did not include a teaching and/or application component. Teachers were frustrated that the staff member delivering Hands Off Academy was not using the intervention time to teach the students the social skills needed to keep their hands to themselves. The staff member delivering Hands Off Academy was also frustrated, because she did not know exactly what to teach the students during these sessions. She preferred her traditional approach to talking to the students during these sessions instead of engaging them in intentional learning and practice.

❧❧

How would you address this challenge?

_____

_____

_____

_____

_____

_____

_____

_____

_____

❧❧

Practical solution: The Tier 2 sub-team collaborated with the staff member delivering Hands Off Academy and helped her develop a menu of lesson topics that needed to be addressed during Hands Off Academy sessions. After asking for feedback from the teachers in regards to skills to teach, they worked together on finding behavior lessons and methods of teaching these students the skills they needed to meet their Hands Off Academy goals.

Tool/resource used: Menu of Hands Off Academy Lesson Topics.

Note: Additional Hands Off Academy Lessons and resources are available at the end of this chapter

---

MENU OF HANDS OFF ACADEMY LESSON TOPICS

Session one: Safety skills

Session two: Self-control skills

Session three: Calming down skills

Session four: Personal space skills

Session five: Self regulation skills

Session six: Problem-solving skills

Session seven: Empathy skills

Session eight: Behavior exam

Extra tool/resource used: Behavior lesson websites

BEHAVIOR LESSON WEBSITES

Goleaps.com

Pbisworld.com

Pbischampionmodelsystem.com

shmoop.com

Extra tool/resource used: Hands Off Academy Lesson Template
Note: Additional Hands Off Academy Lessons and resources are available
at the end of this chapter.

Focus Behavior: Self-Control	
Skill: Self-control skill—Learn how to identify body symptoms when they begin to get angry	**Context:** In unstructured settings, students in this Tier 2 intervention are having difficulty keeping their hands to themselves when they perceive a situation to be unfair.

Rationale: Students need the skills necessary for identifying when they are beginning to get angry.

Lesson Steps:

1. Tier 2 intervention staff leading the intervention lesson will share how she feels when she is beginning to get angry (e.g., heart beating fast, pacing, body feeling hot, seeing red).

2. She has students identify what they feel when they are beginning to get angry.

3. She teaches students how to take deep breaths as soon as they notice their identified symptoms and stop and think before they act. She asks them to try taking 10 deep breaths and imagine a stop sign in their head.

4. She has students identify when they have been angry and provide an example and a non-example of how to respond based on their learned skills (taking deep breaths and using the stop-and-think strategy).

Visual signal/cue to use replacement behavior: Visualize a stop sign in their heads when they feel their identified symptoms of anger. Once they see the stop sign or feel the symptoms, they will practice using their deep breathing and stop-and think-skills.

Review: Review skills with students. Check for understanding.

Behavior homework: Students will write a one-page reflection on how they used these skills.

Supplemental activities: Safe role-playing if time permits

Extra tool/resource used: Behavior Exam Sample

Behavior Exam—Hands Off Academy

Answer the following questions on another piece of paper or using a word-processing program:

1. What was the behavior that resulted in your receiving Hands Off Academy? Describe.

2. Name and define three strategies you learned in Hands Off Academy and provide a description of how you are going to use them in the future.

3. Write a wrong-way scenario about a student having difficulty keeping his/her hands to themselves. Provide an example of what the student could have done instead of hitting/pushing.

4. Develop a contract stating your commitment to using your newly learned skills.

5. Research and develop a slide presentation on the topic of physical disputes and provide five ways to calm yourself down.

6. Present your findings in a 10-minute presentation.

Extra tool/resource used: Example Behavior Reflection Sheet

Name: _____

Being Safe Reflection Sheet

Write a plan on how you can be safer:

_____

_____

_____

_____

What happens when you are not safe?

_____

_____

_____

_____

What makes you a safe person?

_____

_____

_____

_____

Write three school rules that help everyone to be safe.

_____

_____

_____

_____

What consequences should be in place for students who are not acting safely?

_____

_____

_____

_____

Give examples of things that are safe and are not safe:

_____   _____

_____   _____

_____   _____

_____   _____

On the back of this page, make a poster about being safe.

Tier 2 Characteristic 4
Existence of Academic/Behavior Goals/Incentives

Behavior and academic goals are established for this Tier 2 intervention. Students receiving this Tier 2 intervention understand their individual and group goals. Staff understand the purpose and goal of the Tier 2 intervention. Tier 2 incentives are purchased and/or available for this Tier 2 intervention based on student and staff feedback. There is a consistent process for distributing Tier 2 intervention incentives when goals are met and a system to ensure consistency of incentives.

Note

In the next chapter, you will learn how to establish SMART goals for each Tier 2 intervention offered at your school. The reason is that you want to know if the Tier 2 intervention is individually and collectively effective for the students receiving it.

ASSESSING OUR CURRENT STATE: WHERE ARE WE IN RELATION TO THIS TIER 2 CHARACTERISTIC?

Section of the Tier 2 Intervention Snapshot Interview

Tier 2 Characteristic	Evidence of Characteristic	Points 0—Not in Place 1—In Progress 2—In Place With Evidence
Characteristic 4: Existence of Academic/Behavior Goals/Incentives	• A collective behavior/academic goal is established for this Tier 2 intervention. • Individual student behavior/academic goals are established for this Tier 2 intervention. • Students receiving the Tier 2 intervention understand their goals. • Incentives are purchased and/or available for the students based on student and staff feedback. • There is a consistent process for distributing Tier 2 incentives for meeting goals.	Total: ____/2

ൟ

What actions should we take to move our school closer to target on the Tier 2 characteristic?

_____

_____

_____

_____

_____

_____

_____

_____

_____

_____

ൟ

FROM THE FIELD: TIER 2 CHARACTERISTIC 4

Hands Off Academy Tier 2 Intervention Example

Challenge: The Tier 2 sub-team identified that students receiving Hands Off Academy Tier 2 intervention were not consistently given incentives for meeting their SMART goals. They also realized the adults were choosing the incentives for the students instead of allowing the students to choose incentives they would be motivated to work toward.

ൟ

How would you address this challenge?

_____

_____

_____

(Continued)

(Continued)

_____

_____

_____

_____

_____

_____

_____

_____

❧❧❧

Practical solution: As a Tier 2 sub-team, they developed the Hands Off Academy Incentive Monitoring Sheet to help ensure that students who were meeting their goals were given their incentives on a consistent basis. They also surveyed the students on the incentives they would like to work toward to help with buy-in from the students.

Tool/resource used: Hands Off Academy Incentive Monitoring Sheet

Hands Off Academy Incentive Monitoring Sheet (Example)			
Student Name	**Incentive of Choice**	**Week of**	**Did He/She Receive Incentive for Meeting Goals? Yes/No**
Zac	Front of the line lunch pass	March 27–March 31	Yes
Sarah	Spin the Incentive Wheel	March 27–March 31	Yes
Don	Snack shop voucher	March 27–March 31	No—he was absent
Fred	Homework pass	March 27–March 31	Yes

Tier 2 Characteristic 5		

Tier 2 Characteristic 5
Plan for Progress Monitoring/Communication

The Tier 2 intervention has a progress monitoring system in place. Tier 2 intervention data are collected consistently and reviewed at least bi-monthly by the Tier 2 sub-team (*Note: Some smaller schools include all PBIS team members in the Tier 2 discussions*). A process is established that ensures weekly updates on progress are supplied to all stakeholders. A process also exists to give and receive feedback to and from stakeholders on the effectiveness of the intervention.

ASSESSING OUR CURRENT STATE: WHERE ARE WE IN RELATION TO THIS TIER 2 CHARACTERISTIC?

Section of the Tier 2 Intervention Snapshot Interview

Tier 2 Characteristic	Evidence of Characteristic	Points 0—Not In Place 1—In Progress 2—In Place With Evidence
Characteristic 5: Plan for Progress Monitoring/ Communication	• Progress monitoring method is in place. • Progress data from the intervention are shared for bi-monthly Tier 2 sub-team meetings. • A process is established for stakeholders to receive weekly updates on progress and provide feedback.	Total: ____/2

❧ ❧

What actions should we take to move our school closer to target on the Tier 2 characteristic?

_____

_____

_____

_____

_____

_____

_____

_____

_____

_____

❧ ❧

FROM THE FIELD: TIER 2 CHARACTERISTIC 5

Hands Off Academy Tier 2 Intervention Example

Challenge: The PBIS sub-team realized that students receiving Hands Off Academy did not know how to be an active part of their academic and behavior goal monitoring process. They were not clear on the purpose of the intervention or what it would take to meet their goals.

How would you address this challenge?

_____

_____

_____

_____

_____

_____

_____

_____

_____

Practical solution: The PBIS Tier 2 Sub-team developed the Hands Off Academy Self Monitoring Form that is used at the beginning of each Hands Off Academy session to assist students in identifying and reflecting on areas to improve.

Tool/resource used: Hands Off Academy Weekly Self-Monitoring Form

Hands Off Academy—Weekly Self-Monitoring Form

Student name: _____

Behaviors: How well did I . . .	Previous week:
Show respect to adults and students?	Circle one: Good Fair Poor
Keep my hands to myself?	Circle one: Good Fair Poor

What worked for you? _____

What didn't work for you? _____

Contract for this week:

I _____ will work on _____
this week in order to meet my behavior goal.

Administrator signature: _____

Student signature: _____

Teacher signature: _____

OVERVIEW OF CATEGORY B
TIER 2 INTERVENTION SNAPSHOT
INTERVIEW RESULTS: TIER 2 CHARACTERISTICS

Note: Complete this form for each Tier 2 intervention offered at your school.

Tier 2 Intervention Snapshot Interview		
Name of Tier 2 intervention: Number of students receiving this Tier 2 intervention:		
Tier 2 Characteristic	**Evidence of Characteristic**	**Points** **0—Not In Place** **1—In Progress** **2—In Place With Evidence**
Characteristic 1: Existence of Criteria and Timely Referral Process	• Entrance and exit criteria are established. • A clear referral process is in place. • At least 80% of staff understand the criteria and referral process. • Students who meet the criteria are placed in a timely fashion (within a week of referral).	Characteristic 1 point total: ____/2
Characteristic 2: Visibility of Tier 2 Intervention Schedule	• An intervention schedule is created and provided to the stakeholders to reference dates and times of the weekly intervention sessions (6–8 weeks). • The schedule is clear and there is a method to access a copy of the schedule and changes to the schedule as needed. • Student attendance is monitored and communicated based on the schedule.	Characteristic 2 point total: ____/2
Characteristic 3: Evidence of Behavior Lessons and Social Skills	• Behavior lessons and social skills development are utilized during each session. • Behavior lessons and social skills are delivered in a variety of engaging methods. • Students are given opportunities to practice their newly learned social skills.	Characteristic 3 point total: ____/2

Tier 2 Characteristic	Evidence of Characteristic	Points 0—Not In Place 1—In Progress 2—In Place With Evidence
Characteristic 4: Existence of Academic/Behavior Goals/Incentives	• A collective behavior/academic goal is established for this Tier 2 intervention. • Individual student behavior/academic goals are established for this Tier 2 intervention. • Students receiving the Tier 2 intervention understand their goals. • Incentives are purchased and/or available for the students based on student and staff feedback. • There is a consistent process for distributing Tier 2 incentives for meeting goals.	Characteristic 4 point total: _____/2
Characteristic 5: Plan for Progress Monitoring/ Communication	• Progress monitoring method is in place • Progress data from the intervention are shared for bi-monthly Tier 2 sub-team meetings. • A process is established for stakeholders to receive weekly updates on progress and provide feedback.	Characteristic 5 point total: _____/2

Additional observations:	Total Score: _____/10 Overall scoring guide

On Target	8–10 total Points
Making Progress	4-7 total points
Needs Improvement	0–3 total points

Bonus Section
Hands Off Academy Intervention

In this section, you will find the definition of Hands Off Academy and exercises/lessons utilized during Hands Off Academy Tier 2 intervention for your reference. For every Tier 2 behavior intervention, the following need to be present for successful implementation: identifying function/goal setting, teaching needed skills, opportunity for application and practice, and demonstration of mastery. See this example of Hands Off Academy as a reference.

What is Hands Off Academy?

Hands Off Academy is a targeted/at risk Tier 2 intervention designed to teach students demonstrating at-risk behaviors with aggression the problem-solving skills needed to keep their hands to themselves. During Hands Off Academy sessions, students receive instruction and engage in exercises to help them learn replacement behaviors and practice them in real-life settings. In addition, goals are monitored throughout Hands Off Academy by the students and the adults implementing the intervention. In this section, you will find samples of exercises utilized in Hands Off Academy.

HANDS OFF ACADEMY ENTRY INTERVIEW

1. Why do you think you are enrolled in Hands Off Academy?

2. What skills do you think you need that will help you keep your hands to yourself?

3. What makes you angry enough to put your hands on others?

4. Describe a time when you put your hands on someone when you were mad.

5. What was the consequence of that action?

6. What could you have done instead?

7. What do you think your goals should be for participating in this intervention?

8. What are some things you like to do for fun?

9. What is a possible incentive you would like to work for?

10. Who is an adult on campus you connect with and respect?

11. Why do you resort to using your hands when you are upset?

Hands Off Academy Goal Setting and Self Monitoring Sheet		
What is my overall behavior goal in Hands Off Academy?		
What actions am I going to take to meet this goal?		
What is my overall academic goal in Hands Off Academy?		
What actions am I going to take to meet this goal?		
Weekly Self monitoring: How did I do with my goals?		
Week 1	Behavior	If I did not meet my goals, what actions am I going to take to meet them next week?
	Academic	
Week 2	Behavior	If I did not meet my goals, what actions am I going to take to meet them next week?
	Academic	
Week 3	Behavior	If I did not meet my goals, what actions am I going to take to meet them next week?
	Academic	
Week 4	Behavior	If I did not meet my goals, what actions am I going to take to meet them next week?
	Academic	
Week 5	Behavior	If I did not meet my goals, what actions am I going to take to meet them next week?
	Academic	
Week 6	Behavior	If I did not meet my goals, what actions am I going to take to meet them next week?
	Academic	
Week 7	Behavior	If I did not meet my goals, what actions am I going to take to meet them next week?
	Academic	
Week 8	Behavior	If I did not meet my goals, what actions am I going to take to meet them next week?
	Academic	

HANDS OFF ACADEMY: SELF-CONTROL LESSON

What is the definition of self-control?

What is a good example of demonstrating self-control?

What is an example of not demonstrating self-control?

What are some skills you need to help you demonstrate self-control?

Practice scenario: Phil was wearing his new shoes to school. He had saved up for months to buy them, and when he got to school, Jason was goofing around and accidentally stepped on them. Phil reacted by pushing Jason repeatedly until the administrator noticed and stopped him.

How should Phil have reacted?

How could he have demonstrated self-control?

What advice would you give Phil?

Practice scenario rewrite: Rewrite Phil's story below, by applying your newly learned self-control skills. What could he have done instead?

_____

_____

_____

_____

_____

_____

_____

_____

_____

_____

List three ways you are going to practice showing self-control this week. Be prepared to share when you used these skills during the next session.

1.

2.

3.

I commit to practicing my new skills this week:

Signature _____

HANDS OFF ACADEMY: CALMING DOWN LESSON

What is the definition of calming down?

What is a good example of demonstrating how to calm down when you are mad or upset?

What is an example of not demonstrating how to calm down when you are mad or upset?

What are some skills you need that will help you calm down when you are mad or upset?

Practice scenario: Jennifer and Dave broke up because Dave told her he liked another girl named Fera. Jennifer was so mad at Fera she posted mean messages about her all over social media. The next day at school, Jennifer approached Fera in the restroom and began pushing her and pulling her hair.

How should Jennifer have reacted?

How could she have demonstrated calming down?

What advice would you give Jennifer?

Practice scenario rewrite: Rewrite Jennifer's story below by applying your newly learned calming down skills. What could she have done instead?

_____

_____

_____

_____

_____

_____

_____

_____

List three ways you are going to practice calming down when you are mad or upset. Be prepared to share when you practiced these skills during next session.

1.

2.

3.

I commit to practicing my new skills this week:

Signature _____

HANDS OFF ACADEMY: PROBLEM-SOLVING LESSON

What is the definition of problem-solving?

What is a good example of demonstrating how to problem solve when you are mad or upset?

What is an example of not demonstrating problem-solving when you are mad or upset?

What are some skills you need to help you demonstrate problem-solving when you are mad or upset?

Practice scenario: Kyle was mad at Max because of a disagreement during a soccer game about the rules. Kyle approached Max in the locker room and punched him on his arm.

How should Kyle have reacted?

How could he have demonstrated problem-solving skills?

What advice would you give Kyle?

Practice scenario rewrite: Rewrite Kyle's story below by applying your newly learned problem-solving skills. What could he have done instead?

_____

_____

_____

_____

_____

_____

_____

_____

_____

_____

List three ways you are going to practice problem solving when you are mad or upset this week? Be prepared to share when you practiced these skills during next session.

1.

2.

3.

I commit to practicing my new skills this week:

Signature _____

HANDS OFF ACADEMY: EMPATHY LESSON

What is the definition of empathy?

What is a good example of demonstrating empathy?

What is an example of not demonstrating empathy?

What are some skills you need to help you demonstrate empathy?

Practice scenario: Sam was considered to be a bully at school. He would go around hitting and pushing other students in order to entertain his friends. One student in particular was so affected by Sam that he refused to come to school.

How should Sam behave at school?

How could he demonstrate empathy toward other students?

What advice would you give Sam?

Practice scenario rewrite: Rewrite Sam's story below by applying your newly learned empathy skills. What could he do instead?

_____

_____

_____

_____

_____

_____

_____

_____

_____

_____

List three ways you are going to practice showing empathy this week? Be prepared to share when you practiced these skills during next session.

1.

2.

3.

I commit to practicing my new skills this week:

Signature_____

HANDS OFF ACADEMY FINAL PROJECT

Research what happens to adults if they resort to hands-on behaviors.

What are the consequences for adults if they use physical means to solve problems?

What does the law say about using physical means?

Identify a case where someone got into trouble because they put their hands on somebody else. What could this person have done instead?

Research ways to teach other students how to keep their hands to themselves.

Prepare a 10-slide presentation with strategies students could use instead of putting their hands on others.

Present this presentation in three classrooms.

Write a two-page essay about this experience.

HANDS OFF ACADEMY BEHAVIOR EXAM

What does it mean to keep your hands to yourself?

What is the definition of self-control? Provide an example of a student not demonstrating self-control and then provide suggestions for the student to improve his/her behavior.

What is the definition of calming down? Provide an example of a student not demonstrating how to calm down when he/she is mad or upset, and then provide suggestions for the student to improve his/her behavior.

What is the definition of empathy? Provide an example of a student not demonstrating empathy and then provide suggestions for the student to improve his/her behavior.

Provide three examples of when you have utilized your newly learned skills.

Write a contract stating how you are going to continue using these skills and keep your hands to yourself.

Develop a project you will complete that will include a service learning component. Define the steps of the project.

Getting Started With Category C— Tier 2 Academic and Behavior SMART Goals and the Work of the PBIS Tier 2 Sub-Team

This section of the book focuses on the continued development of a Champion Model PBIS System at the Silver Level; specifically, this chapter will allow you to establish Tier 2 academic and behavioral goals and the actions of a school's PBIS Tier 2 sub-team to support this work. We have found most schools typically establish Tier 1 school-wide academic and behavior goals as a part of their regular school accountability plans. However, we rarely find behavior goals aligned with each Tier 2 intervention provided at the school. How can you monitor for effectiveness without goals present? You can't. Your Tier 2 sub-team must set goals that are monitored to see if the Tier 2 interventions provided are working. One critical role of the Tier 2 sub-team is to set and evaluate these Tier 2 intervention goals on at least a bi-monthly basis. Reviewing goals and progress should be a standing agenda item in every Tier 2 sub-team meeting. It is important to note there are two levels of goal setting: for each Tier 2 intervention offered at your school *Level 1* goals are the **collective** Tier 2 intervention academic and behavior goals (e.g., set goals based on the common areas students are working on academically and behaviorally to see if the majority of the students in the Tier 2 intervention are responding and meeting their collective goals); *Level 2* goals are the **individual** student Tier 2 intervention goals (e.g., set individual goals based on the needs of each individual student; therefore, if the Tier 2 intervention collective goals are not met, students who are responding and making progress are not missed). The Tier 2 intervention goals provided in this section are Level 1 goal examples, which are collective in nature. It is critical that the Tier 2 sub-team review these goals with up-to-date data for each Tier 2 intervention offered at the school at least bi-monthly during Tier 2 sub-team meetings. This will allow for modifications and adjustments necessary based on data and stakeholder input.

For the purpose of attaining PBIS Silver Champion level status, your school needs to demonstrate effectiveness of one Tier 2 intervention offered at your school. Data evidence of meeting academic and behavior SMART goals at the collective level for that particular Tier 2 intervention should be demonstrated.

TIP: *It is important for us to note the best practice is that you have established SMART goals aligned to every Tier 2 intervention offered at your school. As your sub-team builds its capacity to design and monitor Tier 2 interventions and goals effectively, it is recommended to develop collective academic and behavior goals for each Tier 2 intervention at your school.*

Note

We receive many questions asking why academic goals are connected to each Tier 2 intervention. In short, we believe that everything we do socially and emotionally is to also support the academic success of each student; therefore, it is necessary to make a connection between academics and behavior in the goals.

CRITICAL TAKEAWAYS

- *In Chapter 3, you learned how to develop a system that supports implementation of Tier 2 interventions. And in Chapter 4, you learned how to utilize the five Tier 2 characteristics to help you audit each Tier 2 intervention offered at your school.*
- *In this chapter you will learn how to establish and monitor collective academic and behavior SMART goals for each Tier 2 intervention offered at your school. Essentially, you are evaluating the effectiveness of your Tier 2 behavior interventions.*
- *We recommend these SMART goals be monitored by the Tier 2 PBIS sub-team on (at minimum) a bi-monthly basis. It is essential to review the data from these Tier 2 interventions to determine which students are in need of additional supports for their academic and behavioral success.*
- *To reiterate, in Chapter 3 you learned how to build the foundation to support the Tier 2 interventions provided at your school; in Chapter 4, you learned how to design and audit essential characteristics necessary for effective Tier 2 interventions; and in this chapter, you will learn how to establish and monitor collective SMART goals for every Tier 2 intervention provided at your school.*

So why have an academic and behavior SMART goal for each Tier 2 intervention at the school?

Tier 2 interventions are designed to help students receive targeted behavioral supports needed to access their education. So ultimately, improving or maintaining academics for students receiving Tier 2 interventions is one strong indicator of whether or not the implemented Tier 2 intervention is effective. Additionally, having academic and behavior SMART goals aligned with each Tier 2 intervention will help the PBIS Tier 2 sub-team monitor progress on an at least bi-monthly basis and share this information with stakeholders.

Important Note: The Tier 2 academic SMART goal can be designed to address the entire group of students receiving the Tier 2 targeted/at-risk intervention collectively (e.g., students receiving Hands Off Academy will achieve or maintain a C average) or individually target Tier 2 targeted/at-risk intervention goals (e.g., students receiving Hands Off Academy will meet their individual academic goals). We suggest that collective and individual goals be set for students receiving Tier 2 interventions at your school, but to begin, we suggest the collective approach. This way, if collectively students are not meeting their goals, then the Tier 2 intervention is not working. However, if the majority of the students in a particular Tier 2 intervention are meeting their goals, it is essential to begin taking a closer look at the individual goals of the students not meeting the collective goals of the group.

One must demonstrate positive change in academic and behavioral outcomes aligned with one PBIS Tier 2 targeted/at-risk intervention provided at your school to become a Silver Level PBIS Champion school. Silver Level schools must also have the preceding tier (Tier 1—Bronze Level) firmly established while also achieving academic and behavioral goals in its current tier (Tier 2—Silver Level):

- Tier 1: The Bronze Level requires at least one ***school-wide*** academic and behavioral SMART goal to be established and achieved. (See *The PBIS Tier One Handbook* as a reference.)
- Tier 2: The Silver Level requires that the Tier 1 goals are met with at least one ***targeted/at-risk*** Tier 2 intervention academic and behavioral collective SMART goal established and achieved for students.
- Tier 3: The Gold Level requires that the Tier 1 and Tier 2 goals are met, and ***individualized*** academic and behavioral SMART goals are established and achieved for students not responding to Tier 1 and Tier 2 interventions (in both the general education and special education settings).

So what is a Tier 2 intervention academic goal? A Tier 2 academic goal is a targeted/at-risk intervention academic SMART (Strategic and Specific, Measurable, Attainable/Achievable, Results-Oriented and Relevant, and Time-Bound) goal drafted by the PBIS Tier 2 sub-team based on targeted/at-risk academic data of the students participating in each Tier 2 intervention at the school.

So what is a Tier 2 intervention behavioral goal? A Tier 2 behavior goal is a targeted/at-risk intervention SMART goal drafted by the PBIS Tier 2 sub-team based on targeted/at-risk behavioral data of the students participating in each Tier 2 intervention at the school.

A PBIS Champion Model uses multiple data sources to establish at least one Tier 2 intervention academic goal and Tier 2 intervention behavior goal, develops actions directly aligned toward achieving established goals, executes the actions, then monitors and communicates progress toward achieving the goals.

In this chapter, we will provide a series of questions for you to consider as you reflect on your Tier 2 systems and an action plan template to support future work as well as a Tier 2 academic and behavioral goals questionnaire. The questionnaire should be used to assess the current state of your selected Tier 2 intervention relative to academic and behavioral goals. The action plan template can be used to help plan, execute, and monitor next-step, high-leverage systems work. The important aspect of Category C is that your system establishes at least one Tier 2 intervention academic goal and one behavioral goal that includes specific indicators of success, develops actions directly aligned to those goals, executes the actions, then monitors progress toward goal attainment. This should be a focus for the PBIS Tier 2 sub-team—to lead this work.

Who should complete the questionnaire? The PBIS Tier 2 sub-team should complete the questionnaire. If you do not have a PBIS Tier 2 sub-team established just yet, the PBIS team should complete the questionnaire.

Tier 2 Intervention Name: _____		
Tier 2 Academic and Behavioral Goals Questionnaire		
Questions to Consider	**Academic** **Yes or No**	**Behavioral** **Yes or No**
1. Does our school have a PBIS Tier 2 sub-team that reviews Tier 2 intervention academic/behavioral data?		
2. Does our PBIS Tier 2 sub-team meet at least twice a month to review Tier 2 intervention academic/behavioral data?		
3. Does our PBIS Tier 2 sub-team have access to Tier 2 intervention academic/behavioral data?		
4. Has our PBIS Tier 2 sub-team established at least one Tier 2 intervention academic/behavioral SMART goal based on assessed need?		
5. Can every PBIS Tier 2 sub-team member at our school articulate our Tier 2 intervention academic/behavioral SMART goals?		
6. Does our school have a process to monitor progress toward meeting our established Tier 2 intervention academic/ behavioral SMART goals?		
7. Does our school have a plan to communicate progress made on Tier 2 intervention academic/behavioral SMART goals to our staff and stakeholders?		
8. Does our school PBIS Tier 2 sub-team use an agenda that focuses discussion on our Tier 2 academic/behavioral SMART goals?		

TIER 2 Intervention
Academic and Behavioral Goals
Actions to Consider Based on Data Analysis

- Establish a PBIS Tier 2 sub-team that reviews Tier 2 intervention academic and behavioral data.
- Calendar the PBIS Tier 2 sub-team to meet at least twice a month to review Tier 2 academic and behavioral data.
- Use the baseline academic and behavioral data from students in the Tier 2 intervention to establish a collective Tier 2 intervention goal for both academics and behavior.

Note: *It is important to have a collective purpose and outcome for offering the Tier 2 intervention (e.g., improving grades, mastering standards, decreasing suspension days, improving task completion, improving social skills, improving motivation, etc.).*

- Administration or selected Tier 2 intervention lead provides the Tier 2 sub-team access to Tier 2 intervention academic and behavioral data and prepares and provides reports requested by the PBIS Tier 2 sub-team at every meeting.

Note: *The administration supports this lead member with resources and protected time to organize Tier 2 intervention information.*

- PBIS Tier 2 sub-team develops at least one Tier 2 academic and behavioral SMART goal (including indicators of success) based on Tier 2 data and stakeholder input.
- PBIS Tier 2 sub-team regularly (every staff meeting) has a designated time to educate and update the rest of staff on Tier 2 intervention progress.
- The PBIS Tier 2 sub-team invites students to come speak to staff about their Tier 2 intervention experiences.
- PBIS Tier 2 sub-team establishes a process and schedule to monitor the Tier 2 intervention academic and behavioral goals (bi-monthly, quarterly, by semester, yearly).
- PBIS Tier 2 sub-team selects and uses an agenda or documentation memory log of their preference to log progress of the (academic and behavioral) SMART goals and next steps.
- Gather input and feedback from students, staff, and other stakeholders regarding the focus of targeted/at-risk intervention academic and behavioral goals.
- Build staff knowledge of the *why* and *how* of implementing Tier 2 interventions in support of achieving targeted/at-risk intervention academic and behavioral SMART goals.
- Keep the targeted/at-risk academic and behavioral SMART goals a priority (e.g., write them into your school site plan, post them on the PBIS Data Wall, etc.).

Analyze your Tier 2 Intervention Academic and Behavioral Goals Questionnaire data. What did the data tell you? Based on the information gained from this analysis and the suggested actions to consider, what next-step or high-leverage actions will your PBIS Tier 2 sub-team take in support of the work—which is to establish at least one Tier 2 intervention academic and behavioral SMART goal that includes specific indicators of success, develop directly aligned actions to accomplish those goals, execute actions, and monitor progress toward goal attainment?

⋙⋘

Actions:

For each action, state when the action will start, person(s) responsible, evidence of the action, and the target completion date. As you monitor these actions, include the date as each is completed.

Action	Timeline (month and year to start action)	Person(s) Responsible	Evidence	Target Completion Date (month/year)	Actual Completion Date (month/year)
1.					
2.					
3.					
4.					

If your system has already established a Tier 2 intervention academic goal and a Tier 2 intervention behavioral goal, then use the following tools (Comparing Our Tier 2 Intervention Academic Goal With SMART Goal Characteristics and Comparing Our Tier 2 Intervention Behavioral Goal With SMART Goal Characteristics) to compare your goals with SMART goal criteria. If your system does not have Tier 2 intervention goals set in one or both of these areas (academic and behavioral), use the SMART criteria to establish your goals.

COMPARING OUR TIER 2 INTERVENTION ACADEMIC GOAL WITH SMART GOAL CHARACTERISTICS

Does our academic goal have each of the following characteristics?

Strategic and **S**pecific

Measurable

Attainable/**A**chievable

Results-Oriented and **R**elevant

Time-Bound

SAMPLE: Hands Off Academy Tier 2 Intervention Academic SMART Goal:

Comparing a Tier 2 Intervention Academic Goal With SMART Goal Characteristics

SMART Goal Characteristics	Our Tier 2 Intervention Academic Goal: Write your targeted/at-risk academic goal.
	By the end of the 8th week of participating in the Hands Off Academy Tier 2 intervention, at least 3 out of 5 students will demonstrate a C average in GPA when compared to the baseline GPA 8 weeks prior to beginning this intervention. *Note: Baseline data prior to Hands Off Academy is below a C average.*
Strategic and Specific	*By the end of the 8th week, at least 3 out of 5 students will demonstrate a C average in GPA when compared to the baseline GPA data 8 weeks prior to beginning this intervention.*

Strategic and Specific (continued)	*Research has found there is a correlation between academic difficulties and acting-out behavior. Students who are suspended or expelled from school tend to do worse academically over time than students who do not struggle academically. We believe the more proactive we are in helping students academically, the greater the likelihood that we will increase positive behavior outcomes for our students.*
Measurable	*The 8 weeks prior to the intervention GPA of the students is compared to 8 weeks after the intervention GPA. We have the baseline data (all 5 students have a below C average GPA) and a data collection system that will give us the end of the 8-week data.*
Attainable/ Achievable	*Baseline data: All 5 students have a below C average GPA. We know what our baseline data are and believe with the implementation of Hands Off Academy Tier 2 intervention a C average GPA in at least 3 out of 5 students after the 8 weeks is attainable. The weekly check-in and monitoring system will help the students stay accountable for their academic performance.*
Results- Oriented and Relevant	*Results-oriented—At least 3 out of 5 students will have no lower than a C average GPA when compared to 8 weeks prior to beginning the intervention GPA.* *Relevant—Multi-Tiered Systems of Support (MTSS) is a framework designed to help provide tiered levels of support behaviorally and academically for all students. This includes teaching behavior similar to academics.*
Time-Bound	*By the end of the 8 weeks of intervention.*

PRACTICE: Use the Blank Template Below With Your PBIS Tier 2 Sub-Team to Establish Your Tier 2 Intervention Academic Goal.

SMART Goal Characteristics	Our Tier 2 Intervention Academic Goal: Write your Tier 2 intervention academic goal.
Strategic and Specific	Write the portion of your Tier 2 intervention academic goal evidencing that it is strategic and specific.
Measurable	Write the portion of your Tier 2 intervention academic goal evidencing that it is measurable.
Attainable/ Achievable	Explain why you believe your Tier 2 intervention academic goal is attainable/achievable.
Results- Oriented and Relevant	Write the portion of your Tier 2 intervention academic goal with evidence that it is results-oriented and relevant.
Time-Bound	Write the portion of your Tier 2 intervention academic goal evidencing that it is time bound.

❧❧

The final version of our Tier 2 intervention academic SMART goal is . . .

_____

_____

_____

_____

_____

_____

_____

_____

_____

❧❧

COMPARING OUR TIER 2 INTERVENTION BEHAVIORAL GOAL WITH SMART GOAL CHARACTERISTICS

Does our behavior goal have each of the following characteristics?

Strategic and **S**pecific

Measurable

Attainable/**A**chievable

Results-Oriented and **R**elevant

Time-Bound

SAMPLE: Hands Off Academy Tier 2 Intervention Behavioral SMART Goal:

Comparing a Tier 2 Intervention Behavioral Goal With SMART Goal Characteristics

SMART Goal Characteristics	Our Tier 2 Intervention Behavioral Goal: Write your Tier 2 behavioral goal.
	By the end of the 8th week of participating in the Hands Off Academy Tier 2 intervention, at least 3 out of 5 students will demonstrate a decreased number of suspensions by at least 50 percent when compared to the baseline data 8 weeks prior to beginning this intervention. *Note: Baseline data prior to Hands Off Academy is 3 suspension days for hands-on behavior per student (5 students—total 15 suspension days)*
Strategic and Specific	*By the end of the 8th week, at least 3 out of 5 students will demonstrate a decreased number of suspension days by at least 50 percent when compared to the baseline suspension data 8 weeks prior to beginning this intervention.* *Research has found that students who are suspended or expelled from school tend to do worse behaviorally over time than students who comply with school rules. We believe the more proactive we are in teaching skills the students are lacking, the greater the likelihood we will increase positive behavioral outcomes for our students.*
Measurable	*The suspension data 8 weeks prior to the intervention is compared to 8 weeks after the intervention suspension data. We have the baseline data (15 suspensions total prior to the intervention: 3 suspension days per student for hands-on behavior) and a data collection system that will give us the end of the 8-week data.*
Attainable/ Achievable	*Baseline data: 15 suspensions.* *We know what our baseline data are and believe with the implementation of Hands Off Academy Tier 2 intervention a 50 percent decrease in suspension days in at least 3 out of 5 students after the 8 weeks is attainable.*
Results Oriented and Relevant	*Results-oriented: 50 percent decrease in suspension days in at least 3 out of 5 students compared to 8 weeks prior to beginning the intervention suspension data.* *Relevant: Research has found that students who were suspended and/ or expelled—particularly those who were repeatedly disciplined—were more likely to be held back a grade or drop out of school than students not involved in the disciplinary system. When a student was suspended or expelled, his or her likelihood of being involved in the juvenile justice system the subsequent year increased significantly.*

(Continued)

(Continued)

Results Oriented and Relevant (continued)	*Multi-Tiered Systems of Support (MTSS) is a framework designed to provide tiered levels of support behaviorally and academically for all students. This includes teaching behavior in ways similar to teaching academics.*
	Federal guidelines for schools to improve school climate and discipline include the following: creating positive climates and focus on prevention; developing clear, appropriate, and consistent expectations and consequences to address disruptive student behaviors (improve behavior, increase engagement, boost achievement); and ensuring fairness, equity, and continuous improvement.
	The Local Control Accountability Plan (LCAP) highlights school climate and connectedness through a variety of factors, such as suspension and expulsion rates and other locally identified means.
Time-Bound	*By the end of the 8 weeks of intervention.*

PRACTICE: Use the Blank Template Below With Your PBIS Tier 2 Sub-Team to Establish Your Tier 2 Intervention Behavioral Goal.

SMART Goal Characteristics	Our Tier 2 Intervention Behavioral Goal: Write your Tier 2 intervention behavioral goal.
Strategic and Specific	Write the portion of your Tier 2 intervention behavioral goal evidencing that it is strategic and specific.
Measurable	Write the portion of your Tier 2 intervention behavioral goal evidencing that it is measurable.
Attainable/ Achievable	Explain why you believe your Tier 2 intervention behavioral goal is attainable/achievable.
Results-Oriented and Relevant	Write the portion of your Tier 2 intervention behavioral goal evidencing that it is results-oriented and relevant.
Time-Bound	Write the portion of your Tier 2 intervention behavioral goal evidencing that it is time-bound.

The final version of our Tier 2 intervention behavioral SMART goal is . . .

_____

_____

_____

_____

_____

_____

_____

_____

_____

Part III
What Next?

Tier 2 Lessons Learned, Case Studies, and Bringing It All Together

This chapter begins with a few lessons learned from educators who have been trained in the development of our Positive Behavior Interventions and Supports (PBIS) Champion Model System, representing more than 400 schools. Next, four case studies from various educational settings (elementary school, middle school, high school, and an alternative education school) are presented; all four schools have been recognized as Silver PBIS Champion Model Schools. The case studies focus on some of the challenges these schools faced and the actions they took to move their system to a Tier 2 Silver PBIS Champion Model. This chapter concludes with the opportunity for you to bring it all together and make sense of your current context and decide on your next course of action.

CASE STUDIES

As you read these case studies, reflect on the ABCs of developing a Tier 2 Silver PBIS Champion Model: Category A—8 PBIS Tier 2 markers, Category B—5 Tier 2 characteristics, and Category C—Tier 2 academic and behavioral goals and the work of the PBIS Tier 2 sub-team. These schools faced various challenges, and the leadership (administrative, teacher, and support staff) took specific actions to move the school from its current state to a more desired future—recognized as a Tier 2 Silver Champion Model School. Consider the following focus questions as you read and reflect on each case:

> What specific actions were taken that supported the development of a strong PBIS Tier 2 foundation?
>
> What category did these actions address (A, B, or C)?
>
> What actions might you consider a *red flag* and indicate that something may need to be addressed?

Lessons Learned
• Administrator attendance at all PBIS Tier 2 sub-team meetings is essential. The PBIS Tier 2 sub-team members feel like their ideas are supported and heard.
• All members of the PBIS Tier 2 sub-team must deliver consistent key messages regarding offered Tier 2 interventions—common language must be used.
• When alternative discipline is used appropriately and communication with staff about discipline decisions for students receiving Tier 2 interventions is timely, staff commitment is strengthened and sustained.
• When the PBIS Tier 2 sub-team holds itself accountable for its action plan steps, students and staff experience consistent implementation and follow-through.
• Feedback must be gathered on a regular, ongoing basis from stakeholders to maximize PBIS Tier 2 intervention implementation success and gain commitment from all.
• The allocation of protected time for the PBIS sub-team to meet at least twice a month is essential for consistent implementation and staff messaging about progress.
• Establishing targeted/at-risk intervention academic and behavioral SMART goals is essential to the evaluation of a PBIS Tier 2 system and its effectiveness.
• Taking the time to educate stakeholders on Tier 2 interventions is key to implementation success.
• Allocate funds for Tier 2 incentives.

ELEMENTARY SCHOOL CASE STUDY:
CHECK-IN CHECK-OUT (CICO) TIER 2 INTERVENTION

WILLOW ELEMENTARY SCHOOL

Willow Elementary School offered a Tier 2 intervention called Check-In Check-Out (CICO). This intervention was designed to help check in with students demonstrating repeated minor behaviors in class but who were responsive to adult interactions. When the school first began with this intervention, they did not have a system in place to teach students how to earn their CICO points, and the teachers did not know the purpose behind CICO. In addition, there were 25 students in this intervention and no one to monitor its implementation. The office staff were frustrated, because they had students coming in and out of the office at inconsistent times throughout the day without procedures that everyone agreed upon. Some additional challenges included teachers not filling out the forms, students not checking in or out, and poor follow-through on incentives for students who met their goals. Additionally, a process did not exist in the event that a teacher was off campus or unavailable to help their student continue meeting their goal and carry out the intervention. Some teachers began referring to this intervention as "psycho," mocking the acronym (CICO), which also demonstrated a lack of buy-in from the teachers.

The PBIS Tier 2 sub-team (a small subgroup of the school's PBIS team) was established to help tighten this Tier 2 intervention. The Tier 2 sub-team comprised the school administrator, the school psychologist, and the CICO lead teacher. They added the following components to improve this intervention:

- They set up Tier 2 intervention meetings at least twice a month to evaluate the effectiveness of CICO.
- They designed a CICO training to educate the staff on the purpose of CICO.
- They gathered feedback from staff during a staff meeting on what students they believed would respond to a CICO system.
- They set up criteria to enter the intervention; criteria were three to four minor classroom referrals for a repeated behavior impacting academic performance in class.
- They looked at the list of students they currently had in CICO and reviewed behavior and academic data for each student to see if this intervention was appropriate for them. They ended up selecting 10 students from K–6th grade who were appropriate for the intervention.
- Students who were demonstrating other behaviors and needed a different intervention or possibly a Tier 3 intervention were removed from CICO.

- The lead teacher in the Tier 2 PBIS sub-team was relieved from all other adjunct duties. Her adjunct was making sure CICO was taking place. In addition, her before-school or after-school supervision was covered. Her role before and after school was to make sure she checked in and out with the 10 students.
- The office assistant was trained to input the CICO data into a data system. She was provided an hour a week, away from her desk so she was not interrupted, to input the CICO data sheets.
- The administrator made sure the CICO reports were updated weekly and that the data was available for PBIS Tier 2 sub-team meetings.
- The PBIS Tier 2 sub-team also worked with the school psychologist to develop a CICO teaching behavior system. The students received a weekly 30- to 45-minute lesson and skill building for six to eight weeks with the school psychologist. The focus of these sessions was to help students learn the skills they needed to earn their points.
- CICO information was shared with the stakeholders weekly. The parents/guardians also received notice of how the students did daily.
- Incentives were purchased with the support of the PTA (or other budgets) for CICO students. These incentives were specific to what the students receiving CICO requested.
- A backup plan was put into place on days the lead CICO teacher was absent or at another meeting.
- The PBIS Tier 2 sub-team shared CICO data updates to the PBIS team and to all staff at staff meetings and provided an opportunity for teacher feedback.
- They had a few students participating in CICO come and speak to the entire staff about their experience.
- Exit criteria and certificates were established for students who met their CICO goals.
- Some students who met their goals but continued to need the structure were allowed to continue with the form and eventually wean off to a daily check-in, then weekly check-in, and some even became mentors for other students who were beginning CICO.

The school made a lot of growth by putting an intentional focus on the implementation of this CICO intervention. As a result, many students continued to improve academically and behaviorally in their school. Teachers began to notice the positive impact of this intervention once it was implemented with fidelity and their voice was heard throughout the process.

What specific actions were taken that supported the development of a strong PBIS Tier 2 foundation?

_____

_____

_____

_____

_____

What category did these actions address (A, B, or C)?

_____

_____

_____

_____

_____

What actions might you consider a _red flag_ and indicate that something may need to be addressed?

_____

_____

_____

_____

_____

MIDDLE SCHOOL CASE STUDY: PINE MIDDLE SCHOOL

Pine Middle School designed a bullying intervention for a group of girls who continually had difficulty with bullying other girls both in person and online. The way the intervention was originally designed was not effective. The girls were brought together once every two weeks to talk about how things had been going, but there were no compassion-building components, goal setting, or progress monitoring connected to the intervention. As a result, the girls would say what they knew the counselor wanted to hear but then go back to their behaviors of bullying. In order to improve this intervention, the Tier 2 intervention sub-team met to revamp it. Here is how they improved the intervention:

- The students had to meet once a week for at least 30 to 45 minutes with the counselor.
- They had eight behavior sessions to complete and had to meet their goals in order to receive their privileges back (example session topics: goal setting, student interview, compassion building, learning about bullying laws, creating bully prevention exercises and campaigns for the school, self-control skills, how to deal with jealousy, problem-solving skills, tolerance skills, empathy skills).
- They also had to check-in daily with the administrator every morning to remind them to use their new skills.
- The teachers were notified about the skills the girls were working on and were asked to monitor their behaviors in class.
- The girls were told random check-ins were going to take place with the teachers to make sure they were not witnessing any bullying in their classroom. In addition, the supervision staff were also asked to monitor the girls during unstructured times.
- The parents of the girls were notified and asked to monitor their behaviors at home. The girls had behavior homework each week that required them to research or create something to help stop bullying at the school (e.g., one assignment was to develop interview questions about bullying, interview someone who has been bullied, and write a report and suggestions to help stop bullying).
- The PBIS Tier 2 sub-team worked with the school counselor providing the intervention to monitor progress on goals, monitor attendance, and intervene with extra support as needed. They met at least twice a month to review this information and provide feedback to all stakeholders.
- The girls were taught how to self-monitor their goals during each session.

- The girls who met their goals received an incentive of their choice on Friday afternoons (e.g., 30 minutes of free time).
- As the girls consistently met their goals and there were no reports from any stakeholders of their bullying, they were slowly given their privileges back at school.

By holding the girls accountable for their behaviors and providing them with the appropriate skills to problem solve when angry at someone rather than becoming a bully, they made significant growth. One of the six girls did not respond as well as the other girls; she was identified as the ringleader and needed additional intervention and supervision throughout the remainder of the school year. However, the other girls in the intervention noticed (through their newly acquired skills) they were following this person's lead and it was hurting people, so they decided to genuinely change how they treated others.

What specific actions were taken that supported the development of a strong PBIS Tier 2 foundation?

_____

_____

_____

_____

_____

What category did these actions address (A, B, or C)?

_____

_____

_____

_____

_____

(Continued)

(Continued)

What actions might you consider a *red flag* and indicate that something may need to be addressed?

_____

_____

_____

_____

_____

❧ ❧

HIGH SCHOOL CASE STUDY: FIR HIGH SCHOOL

Fir High School attempted to implement a Tier 2 truancy intervention for 20 students who repeatedly were either absent or tardy to school. They established criteria to identify the students (2–3 tardies or absences a week and drop in their GPA). The school counselors decided to meet with the students on their caseload and encourage them to come to school. They met with the students one or two times but became too busy, so the intervention failed. The PBIS Tier 2 sub-team at the school was established to help reestablish this intervention. Here is what they did:

- The PBIS Tier 2 sub-team met with the four school counselors to redesign the truancy intervention.
- Together they created a truancy student interview comprising of questions that would give the counselors a better idea of the function behind why the students were repeatedly late or absent to school.
- They created a truancy student contract that was to be monitored weekly for six to eight weeks with the students.
- The counselors evenly divided up the students (each taking five). They selected students they had already built a relationship with to boost student buy-in.
- They developed a consistent schedule to meet with their group of students and calendared the dates to ensure they met with the students at least weekly (every Monday from 7:45 to 8:15 a.m., students report directly to the counselor).
- Attendance was taken on a shared Google Sheets document and access was given to the other PBIS Tier 2 sub-team members for progress monitoring purposes.

- The counselors worked together to gather baseline academic, attendance, and behavior data of the students to ensure individual and group academic and behavior goals were met.
- The PBIS Tier 2 sub-team worked with the counselors on creating exercises and lessons for each session (e.g., motivation, organization, time management, goal setting, etc.).
- The counselors identified incentives the students wanted to earn if they met their weekly intervention goals (e.g., snack bar credit, lunch fast pass).
- The PBIS Tier 2 sub-team calendared bi-weekly meetings to review student progress.
- Teachers with students in this intervention were notified of the intervention and their student's progress toward their goals. They were also given opportunities to provide input and feedback.

The intentional focus on this intervention made a huge impact for the students and the counselors. They were able to see the positive outcomes connected with establishing and implementing a Tier 2 intervention with fidelity. The majority of the students in the intervention showed improvement in their truancy goals and more than half (15 out of 20) were exited from the intervention after eight weeks for meeting goals; however, they continued to be monitored by their counselors every two weeks. The counselors continued meeting with the students who were exited from the program once a month for a check-in and boost. The five students who did not make adequate progress during the eight weeks remained in the intervention for the remainder of the semester. Meetings were set and their parents/guardians were included to add additional support components for those students.

❧❧❧

What specific actions were taken that supported the development of a strong PBIS Tier 2 foundation?

_____

_____

_____

_____

_____

(Continued)

(Continued)

What category did these actions address (A, B, or C)?

_____

_____

_____

_____

_____

What actions might you consider a *red flag* and indicate that something may need to be addressed?

_____

_____

_____

_____

_____

ALTERNATIVE EDUCATION CASE STUDY: OAK ALTERNATIVE EDUCATION SCHOOL

Oak Alternative Education School was having a difficult time motivating students to complete credits to graduate. The school did not have any interventions in place. Most of the staff assumed their students were in alternative education because no interventions worked. As a result, students were placed in classes and taught in the same manner no matter their effort or skill level. The teachers at the school did not have high expectations for the students. A new administrator who had ten years of alternative education experience as a teacher and administrator was hired to turn around the school. He began by establishing the PBIS team at the school, which included all five teachers and met monthly. As a team, the staff implemented *The PBIS Tier One Handbook* actions to build a foundation for academic and behavioral success. They realized quickly they weren't a school with only students in need of Tier 3 supports. As an alternative education school, they had all three tiers of students to support. As soon as they realized there were different levels of needs at the alternative education school, similar to all other general education schools, they began to see results. After a year of tightening up Tier 1 classroom and unstructured setting systems, they began the planning for Tier 2 interventions at their school. Here is what they did:

- They began by assessing their current state to identify an intervention they could implement at the school. The teachers agreed that lack of motivation to complete credits was a problem for a handful of students.
- They set up criteria for placing students into a Tier 2 motivation intervention; criteria were that the student was one year behind in credits, did not have academic learning difficulties, and was not on track to graduate on time.
- They identified twelve students for this intervention who met the criteria.
- The administrator adjusted one of the teacher's schedules to have a carved-out Tier 2 intervention class with the purpose of helping these six students learn the skills needed to catch up with their credits in their style of preference.
- The identified students were surveyed on their motivation, confidence levels, method of coursework they preferred, and incentives they would like to receive when meeting their goals.
- Students were placed into this Tier 2 intervention class for a quarter. In this class, the teacher utilized one day a week to teach the appropriate skills (academic and social-emotional) to complete the credits. The remaining four days were designed as a structured time for students to work on what they needed to earn their credits.
- The class set a goal together and monitored themselves and the goal weekly.
- The student surveys indicated students preferred an online version of the classes they needed credits for rather than an in-class teaching approach. This allowed for them to work on their class at their own pace with teacher supervision and structure.
- The administrator worked with the county office of education to get access to online classes for the students.
- Skills such as time management, growth mind-set, organization, self-esteem, and confidence were taught in this class using role-playing, scenarios, and opportunities for real-life application of the learned skills.
- On Fridays, students who met their goals were given an incentive of their choice. The incentives were decided with the input of the students (e.g., video game time, free art time, free time to do nothing, homework pass, etc.).
- The students also had a class incentive when everyone in the intervention met their weekly goals for two weeks (e.g., pizza party, extra basketball time, free time).

- Each of the five teachers was provided one half day substitute coverage so they could come sit in the Tier 2 intervention to provide additional input and support suggestions for the students. This helped increase teacher buy-in.
- The PBIS Tier 2 sub-team (which in a small school setting would be the entire teaching staff, administrator, and school psychologist) met twice a month to discuss progress of the students using data and input from all the teachers. Since they already met once a month for Tier 1 actions, they just extended that monthly meeting by 30 minutes to cover Tier 2 and added an additional Tier 2 meeting each month.
- The meetings were calendared and the administrator protected this meeting time.

All six students responded to the intervention. Designing an intervention setting where the students could learn academic and social-emotional skills they were lacking provided an opportunity for students to feel success. However, this took the administrator's support and willingness to innovate to meet the needs of the students rather than doing the same thing these students had not responded to for years (a traditional teaching method).

❧❧

What specific actions were taken that supported the development of a strong PBIS Tier 2 foundation?

_____

_____

_____

_____

_____

What category did these actions address (A, B, or C)?

_____

_____

_____

_____

_____

What actions might you consider a *red flag* and indicate that something may need to be addressed?

_____

_____

_____

_____

_____

BRINGING IT ALL TOGETHER

This book focused on the building blocks of a Tier 2 Silver PBIS Champion Model, otherwise known as the ABCs of Tier 2, designed as an interactive guide to help you assess, learn, process, and action plan your next steps toward Silver Level implementation. Now let's bring it all together.

Tier 2—Silver PBIS Champion Model Progress Summary Sheet		
Category A: Tier 2 markers	What is our score?	What is one action we will employ to make progress in this area? If the highest score was earned, *what will we do to sustain this high level?*
Marker 1: Establish and Operate an Effective PBIS Tier 2 Sub-Team		
Marker 2: Establish and Maintain Tier 2 Staff Commitment		
Marker 3: Establish a Tier 2 Data-Based Process for Identifying Students		
Marker 4: Establish a Tier 2 Data Entry Procedure and Review Plan		
Marker 5: Establish Tier 2 Fidelity Check Process		

(Continued)

(Continued)

Category A: Tier 2 markers (continued)	What is our score?	What is one action we will employ to make progress in this area? If the highest score was earned, *what will we do to sustain this high level?*
Marker 6: Develop and Deliver Tier 2 Lesson Plans		
Marker 7: Establish a Tier 2 Incentive System		
Marker 8: Establish a Tier 2 System for Monitoring and Communicating Progress		
Category B: Tier 2 characteristics	**What is our score?**	**What is one action we will employ to make progress in this area? If the highest score was earned, *what will we do to sustain this high level?***
Characteristic 1: Existence of Criteria and Timely Referral Process		
Characteristic 2: Visibility of Tier 2 Intervention Schedule		
Characteristic 3: Evidence of Behavior Lessons and Social Skills		
Characteristic 4: Existence of Academic/Behavior Goals/Incentives		
Characteristic 5: Plan for Progress Monitoring/Communication		

Category C: Tier 2 academic and behavior SMART goals and the work of the PBIS Tier 2 sub-team	What is our final version of our Tier 2 intervention goals? What is one action we will employ to support progress toward achieving the goal?
Tier 2 academic SMART goal is . . .	
Tier 2 behavior SMART goal is . . .	

Next Steps and Tips for Success

Now that you have had a chance to digest the Tier 2 ABCs necessary to construct an effective Tier 2 behavior system at your school, it is time to practice. *So what is your role as a Tier 2 sub-team?* As a Tier 2 sub-team, you should meet at least twice a month to address the targeted/at-risk student challenges based on your school's data. As a Tier 2 sub-team, your role is to develop, implement, and monitor Tier 2 interventions at your school.

Let's practice: Read the scenarios and work through your first steps in developing a Tier 2 intervention that will address this student challenge. What resources are necessary to implement the Tier 2 intervention? How will you monitor and assess the Tier 2 intervention for effectiveness? Use the Tier 2 markers, Tier 2 characteristics, and Tier 2 SMART goals to help guide your next steps and actions accordingly.

Scenario 1: A group of boys continue to have difficulty keeping their hands to themselves. They are continuously getting into trouble during unstructured time at school. They have been suspended in the past for the same behavior but continue to have difficulties keeping their hands to themselves.

What are your first steps in developing a Tier 2 intervention to help address this student challenge?

What resources are necessary to implement the Tier 2 intervention?

How is the Tier 2 intervention monitored and assessed for effectiveness?

Scenario 2: A group of girls are bullying other students. They are sending mean text messages to other girls during structured and unstructured times. This has been occurring for months, and the girls have been talked to by the administrator several times but continue to engage in this behavior.

What are your first steps in developing a Tier 2 intervention to help address this student challenge?

What resources are necessary to implement the Tier 2 intervention?

How is the Tier 2 intervention monitored and assessed for effectiveness?

Scenario 3: A group of students are regularly sent up to the office for disruptive behaviors in the classroom. The teachers are frustrated and feel like the students are getting away with their behavior. The students have been suspended from class repeatedly but continue with these disruptive behaviors.

What are your first steps in developing a Tier 2 intervention to help address this student challenge?

What resources are necessary to implement the Tier 2 intervention?

How is the Tier 2 intervention monitored and assessed for effectiveness?

Scenario 4: A group of students are failing in school. The teachers indicate a serious lack of motivation. These students are not demonstrating disruptive behaviors; however, work is not getting completed. The students have been talked to by their teachers but continue putting forth no effort.

What are your first steps in developing a Tier 2 intervention to help address this student challenge?

What resources are necessary to implement the Tier 2 intervention?

How is the Tier 2 intervention monitored and assessed for effectiveness?

Scenario 5: (Describe a current scenario based on data at your school)

_____

_____

_____

_____

_____

What are your first steps in developing a Tier 2 intervention to help address this student challenge?

What resources are necessary to implement the Tier 2 intervention?

How is the Tier 2 intervention monitored and assessed for effectiveness?

TIPS FOR SUCCESS

In this section, you will find tips from educators who are implementing the PBIS Champion Model at the Silver Level.

- Keep the school's Tier 1 academic and behavior foundation strong. (Use *The Tier One Handbook* to help.)
- Make sure all administrators at the school are in full support of the implementation of Tier 2 interventions.
- Be intentional about meeting at least twice a month as a Tier 2 sub-team.
- Make sure your support staff are on board for establishing effective Tier 2 systems.
- Create structures that support the implementation of Tier 2 interventions.
- Establish buy-in from the stakeholders.
- Celebrate Tier 2 intervention successes.
- Utilize data to make decisions and problem solve.
- Designate department or staff meeting time to update stakeholders on Tier 2 interventions.
- Be practical but intentional in implementation of Tier 2 interventions.
- Persevere, even if it gets frustrating.
- Be resilient to setbacks and naysayers.
- Keep your focus on what is best for students.

The most impactful tip we can give you is to believe that what you are doing will help at-risk students receive the targeted supports they need to succeed. Understanding your purpose to make an impact on a student's life is critical. You may not see the fruits of your labor initially, but matching the correct intervention with the student, establishing relationships, and following the actions in this book will pay off in the end.

Index

A SAGE Publishing Company

Solutions you want. Experts you trust. Results you need.